ANTONIO SANGIO

THE SYMPTOMS OF
THE SOUL

THE PATH TO THE ORIGIN OF OUR SYMPTOMS
THROUGH REGRESSIVE HYPNOSIS

Copyright ©
No part of this book may be reproduced, scanned or distributed
in any printed or electronic form without the write permission of
Antonio Sangio.

First Edition, 2022
Author's website: www.antoniosangio.com
Cover Design by Rob Williams
Interior Book Design by Antonio Revilla Leyva
Editors: Alejandra Travi Ponce, Juan Pablo León
English Language Editor: Andria Flores

ISBN: 979-8-218-05111-2

To my mother, Rosa Mara Fajardo de Sangio, my first teacher, from whom I learned unconditional love, compassion, and the gift of service. This book is for you.

CONTENTS

INTRODUCTION   11

DEFINITIONS   15
    What is Spirit?
    What is the Soul?
    What is Time?
    Trauma
    The Symptom

THE ILLUSION OF TIME   21
    The Mind and Time
    The Soul and Time
    Multisimultaneity
    The Soul, Trauma, and Time

THE PURPOSE OF THE SOUL   33
    Spirit Groups
    The Guides
    The "Council" of the Elders
    The Library
    Karma
    Contracts
    The Lessons
    The Choice of the Body
    Spiritual Amnesia
    The Hunter
    The Conquistador

SOUL ENTRAPMENT   59
    Types of Entrapment:
    Past Life Entrapment
    The Innocent Mother
    The Girl on the Bus
    Post Mortem Entrapment
    The Young Girl in the Water
    Entrapment in the Womb

    Emma in Her Mother's Womb
    Entrapment During Birth
    The Legless Miner
    Soukaïna in Her Mother's Womb

SOUL FRAGMENTATION   97
    What Symptoms Can a Person With a Fragmented Soul Experience?
    Difference Between Entrapment and Fragmentation of the Soul
    Fragmentation Is One of the Consequences of Entrapment
    The Girl in the Room

TYPES OF DEATH AND THEIR SYMPTOMS   105
    Burned at the Stake
    Falls
    Poisoning
    Buried Alive
    Hanging
    Decapitation
    Suicide
    The Wheat Field
    Thrown From a Balcony
    The Harassed Sailor
    The Sleeping Woman Inside the Coffin
    The Innocent Maid
    The Healer's Heart

THE PERISPIRIT AND BIRTHMARKS   141
    The Perispirit
    Birthmarks

TIMELESS PHRASES   145
    Promises
    Vows
    Pacts
    Oaths
    Curses
    The Last Thought
    The Symptom
    The Therapeutic Approach
    The Curse of the Healer
    I Will Never Leave You

I Will Love You Forever
The Witch

MASCULINE AND FEMININE ENERGY   177
Masculine Energy
Feminine Energy
In Past Lives
During Conception and Pregnancy
During Birth and Early Childhood
Reconciling Energies
Lucy's Disconnection
The Roman Soldier and the Young Woman
The Boy on the Train

RAPE AND MOLESTATION   199
Physical Symptoms
Psychological and Emotional Symptoms
Symptoms at the Energetic and Soul Level
Helping to Complete the Experience
The Slave on the Boat
The Sacrificial Young Woman

THE ROLES WE PLAY IN OUR LIVES   219
The Perpetrator
The Observer
The Village Guard
The Woman Betrayed by the Council

CONCLUSION   235

INTRODUCTION

Since prehistoric times, human beings have wanted to find the origin of the symptoms of a sick body. To do so, he has used various methods and tools to help him understand how they are originated and how to alleviate them. In Ancient Egypt, for example, Imhotep (2630-2611 BC), who was a renowned polymath and inventor, wrote a medical document in which he explained and applied the diagnosis for the treatment of a disease. Similarly, in Babylon, Esagil-kin-apl (1067-1046 BCE), the king's leading scholar, wrote the Diagnostic Handbook, *Sakikkū*, introducing empiricism, logic, and reasoning in the diagnosis of a condition. On the other hand, in the text "Canon of Internal Medicine" of the Yellow Emperor, or Huangdi Neijing, the popular section of basic questions can be found, where the theoretical basis of the methods that Chinese medicine uses for diagnosis is covered.

Other cultures employed different procedures to clarify the cause of symptoms. In ancient Greece, the physician Hippocrates (5th-460th century BC) recorded the relationship between disease and the genetic factor. In the Middle Ages, there were physicians who used different techniques to analyze urine, blood, and pulse. In some cases, they combined these tests with the zodiac and humoral medicine, based on the theory of the four humors that classify people according to their personality traits.

Some schools have focused on treating the symptom only through treatment of the affected organ, regardless of the side effects on the rest of the body. Others have focused on diagnosing and treating the symptom by visualizing the human body as a whole and taking into account the adverse effects on the rest of the organs during the healing process. This would be the case of Western and Chinese medicine.

As for symptoms of a mental nature, for a long time and up to the present day, supernatural factors have been attributed to them, such as demonic possession or to the gods of different cultures. It was precisely this that led certain ancient cultures to practice cranial trepanations and other more modern ones to confine and torture the mentally ill in psychiatric hospitals. Many of these patients have suffered, in one way or another, abuses and injustices in the name of science.

So, if we talk about demonic possessions and their supposed treatments, we would have to mention the Catholic Church and the use of exorcism as a supposed cure. In history, we can find many documented cases of mentally ill people who were exorcised to get rid of supposed entities; on the other hand, shamans of ancient and current cultures see the illness and its symptoms as a type of energetic imbalance that can be associated, among other things, to the loss of the soul. They enter into a trance to enter the spiritual world with the aim of finding the spiritual cause of the condition or to help the soul of the afflicted person to return to the body.

In the 18th century, the German doctor Franz Anton Mesmer, using the concept of animal magnetism (invisible force that all living beings possess), used magnetic passes in the treatment of diseases and their symptoms with interesting results. Mesmer's work and technique was valid for 75 years or so, although we can still find professionals in the health field referring to the so-called mesmerism. In the 19th century, the surgeon James Esdaile, performed hundreds of surgical procedures with the use of hypnosis as anesthesia. In the 20th century, the psychologist and physician Milton Erickson promoted the use of direct suggestions to induce his patients into a deep trance and thus use regression to another age.

By publishing the book *Many Lives, Many Masters* in 1980, the American psychotherapist Brian Weiss transformed the world's view on the use of hypnosis. There, he relates how one of his patients, in a hypnotic state, begins to remember traumas of supposed past lives, which, finally, could give an explanation to her recurrent nightmares and continuous anxiety attacks.

Different cultures at different times have claimed the task of finding relief from what ails human beings. Some approached their diagnosis from an empirical point of view and others from a more scientific one, either treating the symptom in isolation from the rest of the body or from an integral vision, in which the rest of the body and the side effects are taken into account. It is worth mentioning that the latter trend has also opted for treatment from a spiritual point of view, that is, taking the physical body and soul as a whole.

So, who could claim the unique and infallible way to diagnose the diseases that affect the human being? More than once we have seen professionals make mistakes in their diagnosis by relying exclusively on some kind of template for their evaluation. If most professionals use some sort of template or map for diagnosis, does that mean that all human beings are the same and that the same procedure can be used with us all?

If we start with the idea that the soul is the vital energy of the body, that it never dies, and that from the point of view of reincarnation, it has occupied other bodies in previous lives, we will find a series of traumas that it brings from those other bodies to the current one. Just as the subconscious mind leads us to react in a certain way due to the traumas, we have stored in it, the soul does so without any apparent explanation in certain situations, as a result of traumas stored in it that were generated in past lives.

As I explained in my book, *Guiding Lost Souls*, the subconscious mind is not limited to the existence of the body. This information is stored in the soul and can generate in the body all kinds of psychosomatic symptoms, many of them without an apparent scientific logical reason.

Without pretending to be a doctor or a mental health specialist, my goal with this text is to share the concepts that I learned, not only from my teachers Aurelio Mejia and Jose Luis Cabouli, but also that I have found on my own while facilitating hypnosis sessions with my clients. You will be able to appreciate how certain symptoms with no apparent medical explanation were triggered by their soul when facing a scenario or emotion similar to what they experienced in traumas from another life.

In addition, you will be able to clearly see how the symptom works as a thread that leads to the origin of the experience that caused it. It is only a matter of helping the person to make conscious what up to now is unconscious for them, since the traumatic event is not really located in the past. The soul does not understand time. For it, the past is here and now in the present, manifesting itself in the form of symptoms and sensations without any apparent explanation.

I will also share some cases that seem to be taken out of a fiction movie, but that are one hundred percent real and appeared in my practice. They will give you an in-depth understanding of the concept of soul entrapment. Most of the names in these cases have been changed to protect the identity of my clients. Only some of them allowed me to use their real names.

DEFINITIONS

I consider it necessary to define some concepts in order to understand the information that will be shared in the following pages. Although in my book *Guiding Lost Souls* I explain in detail the concepts of spirituality, on this occasion I will make only a brief summary.

What is Spirit?

The word *spirit* comes from the Latin *spiritus*, which means breath, and from the Greek word *pneûma*, which is translated as breath or respiration, referring to the spirit. In the Real Academia de la Lengua Española dictionary we can find the following definitions:

- Immaterial being endowed with reason
- Rational soul
- Generating principle, intimate character, essence or substance of something
- The purest and subtlest part or portion that is extracted from some solid and fluid bodies by means of chemical operations

Throughout history, different cultures and religions have attributed different meanings to the word *spirit*. In the Bible, for example, the following definitions of the word *spirit* can be found: wind, moving air, and breath. In Latin it is known as *spiritus,* and the following references are made:

Genesis 2:7 And the Lord God formed man of the dust of the ground, and breathed into his nostrils the breath of life; and man became a living soul.

In *The Book of Spirits* written by Allan Kardec (Hippolyte Léon Denizard Rivail), spirits are defined as intelligent beings outside of creation—outside of everything we can see and touch—who populate the universe outside of the material world. Spirits are surrounded by a vaporous substance called 'perispirit,' which allows them to hover in the atmosphere and transport themselves wherever they wish.

On the other hand, we can also find contradictory concepts about the spirit, such as that of pure materialism, which says that the spirit is the beginning of organic life and ceases when life ceases. Meanwhile, others maintain that the spirit is the beginning of intelligence of which each being absorbs a small part and returns it to him when life culminates, as if the whole universe had only one spirit.

As can be seen, each culture has a different idea of what the spirit is, thus showing how complicated it is to define it with a single word. How can we specify that which we cannot see or touch? Does our language have the necessary expressions to describe all the characteristics of the soul? If there are still no words to define certain scientific phenomena, how can we pretend to do so with this self-conscious energy?

For purposes of this book, we will take the concept found in *The Spirits' Book*, since it was the author and his collaborators (the spirits themselves) who provided that definition using the limited language of the human being. Spirits are then intelligent beings with their own consciousness who dwell outside of creation, that is to say, who are invisible and reside in the universe.

What is the Soul?

The word *soul* comes from the Latin *anima* and the Greek *psyché*. This first word refers to an entity that, according to some religious and philosophical tendencies, all living beings possess. According to the Latin, this word is also used to designate the principle by which beings are endowed with movement.

If we refer to the Christian religion, for example, man consists of body, spirit and soul, the latter being the one that unifies him as an individual and guides him to perform activities that go beyond the material world.

In Hindu beliefs, reference is made to the transmutation of the soul, an action they called "The Wheel of Samsara" (the cycle of life, death, birth and incarnation), where dharma (actions done for good) and karma (consequence of what has been done), determine the future destiny of each being.

Meanwhile, in *The Spirits' Book*, Allan Kardec shares the answer he got from the mediums when he asked what the soul is:

What is the soul?

"An incarnate spirit."

– What was the soul before its union with a body?

"A spirit."

– Are souls and spirits therefore one and the same thing?

"Yes, souls are no more than spirits. Before uniting with a body, the soul is one of the intelligent beings who populate the invisible world, and it later temporarily assumes a physical envelope in order to purify and enlighten itself."

We are again faced with the challenge of defining in words something we cannot see. This time we will also use the concept provided by the spirits themselves in Allan Kardec's book. When this intelligent energy with its own consciousness is outside the body we will call it spirit, and when it is inside the body, we will call it soul.

What is Time?

This is another concept I have explained in great detail in my book *Guiding Lost Souls*, and I consider it relevant to also include it in this text in order to have a better understanding of what I will share and a better understanding of my clients' experiences during their sessions.

Time can be understood as the way in which the duration or separation of events is measured. In perception through the human brain, time is linear: past, present, and future. This is how we perceive it in the third dimension, which is the one we inhabit. According to the systems theory proposed by the German sociologist Niklas Luhman, time would have a social formation, i.e. it is situated from the perspective of the observer, who makes a distinction between a before and an after.

For the Italian physicist Carlo Rovelli, author of *The Order of Time*, the understanding of time is based on the concept that it has several layers. For him, the great confusion that exists in trying to understand time comes from perceiving all its attributes as a whole, as a single package, when in reality many of these come from mere approximations and implications.

On the other hand, in quantum time, the present, past, and future do not exist because they dissolve into the now. The elementary particles of matter can be in two places or states at once. It is in this quantum universe where the spirits reside, who would be affected by this time, that is, living in the now. It is for this reason that the spirit does not understand time.

Trauma

The word *trauma* comes from the Greek *trauma*, or wound. About it we can find the following definitions:

- Emotional shock that produces lasting damage in the subconscious
- Emotion or negative impression, strong and lasting

From the point of view of spiritual hypnosis, trauma is considered a painful event that the soul has not been able to process completely, physically, emotionally and mentally. Going deeper into this subject, and as we will see later, the consequences of trauma are the entrapment and fragmentation of the soul, which results in one or more symptoms.

The Symptom

The word *symptom* has its origin in the Latin *symptōma*, but in turn comes from a Greek word. If we refer to the dictionary, we will find the following definitions:

- Revealing manifestation of a disease
- Sign or indication that something is happening or is going to happen

From the point of view of spirituality and from my own, a symptom that has no logical or medical explanation is considered to be the result of a traumatic event. The interesting thing to see from this perspective is that the soul does not understand past, present, and future, but only from the now. So, when I say that the symptom is the result of a trauma, I am not only referring to traumas that may have occurred in the present life, but also to those that we experienced while occupying other bodies in past lives.

In the next chapter I will delve a little deeper into the definition of time to understand that time is nothing more than a mere illusion. Understanding time from the point of view of the soul is what allowed me to change my approach to hypnosis sessions.

THE ILLUSION OF TIME

Something we hypnotherapists have difficulty deciphering is how to use the techniques we use in hypnosis sessions with those who come to us. The challenge lies in the fact that both therapists and our patients only know the concept of linear time (past, present, and future). If we say that our hypnosis technique is spiritual, this means that we work with the time that dominates the spirit (the soul): quantum time. Why? Well, because of what we have already explained, because the soul does not understand time, so for the soul everything is happening now.

Once we understand what quantum time is, the approach to therapy changes completely. Knowing that the past is not past, but that it is with us now, allows us to use our techniques in a more effective way. This helps patients make conscious what for them is unconscious and is only manifesting itself in the form of symptoms.

However, this puts us in front of another challenge: navigating (facilitating) the session in linear time, while approaching it from quantum time. I will try to explain this with a short example.

Suppose Jennifer comes in for a session to treat her unexplained fear of the ocean. Every time she goes near the ocean or crosses a bridge that crosses a lake or sea, her body becomes rigid, she has anxiety attacks, and she has trouble breathing. In the pre-session interview, she tells me that she has not had any traumatic experience with the ocean, not even when she was a child.

Already in trance, as we work through the symptoms she describes, Jennifer goes to a past life where she is a man on a Spanish ship being thrown into the ocean for revealing himself. Then, Jennifer, being that man, explains that pre-death experience: his body stiffens as he is restrained and touches the almost frozen ocean, then sinks without being able to breathe.

While it is true that, during the journey through that past life, I guided Jennifer in linear time by saying phrases like "now, go back a little further," and "go to the first time you experienced this," or "I want you to look for a life where you felt these same symptoms," what I was really doing was looking for how that past event related to what she was feeling now. I was also trying to understand what her soul needed to complete in that experience at a physical, emotional, and mental level in order for the symptom to go away, that is, the cause of her soul's entrapment.

After the completion of the past life journey, I told her that I could bring her soul into the light as if it were an event from the past, knowing that her soul was also in Jennifer's body in my office at that moment.

During the whole session I was talking to Jennifer in linear time since that's the way she could understand me, but at the same time I was analyzing the session and choosing the techniques to use from soul time, from now (present time). The main thing was to find out how that traumatic event was related to what she was experiencing in her life as Jennifer and what ended up triggering those symptoms.

A therapist in a spiritual hypnosis session faces multiple challenges, such as speaking in linear time while being, at the same time, a kind of detective looking for past life traumas of the soul. These could be originated during our time in our mother's womb, at birth, in early childhood, or even later in adolescence, youth, or adulthood, however, they must be seen as a whole, as if they were happening now at the same time, since the symptoms are manifesting now.

The Mind and Time

In order to understand that time is just an illusion, I would like to share about the mind and its components. This will also help us understand why people experience what they experience during trance. The mind is understood as a set of faculties with cognitive aspects, such as consciousness, imagination, perception, thought, intelligence, judgment, language, and memory. It also has non-cognitive aspects, such as emotion and instinct.

The mind is composed of the conscious mind and the subconscious mind. The former is our critical part: reason, logic, and willpower. In other words, we could say that the conscious mind is our analytical area. The subconscious mind, on the other hand, is a large repository of negative and positive associations. Everything we have lived through is stored there. For it, time does not exist, and I will explain the reason below.

In the subconscious mind we store associations that dictate and influence the way we behave in life. For example, if in our subconscious mind we have stored the association that a cigarette means relaxation, every time we find ourselves in stressful situations, we will light up a cigarette without even thinking about it. If in our subconscious food is associated with happiness, perhaps because when we were children the only time we were happy was when we went out to eat with our family, then it is most likely that when we feel sad, we will feel the need to eat, even if we are not hungry.

If we remember the song that played on the radio when we fell in love for the first time or the perfume that person wore, we understand that every time we listen to that song or smell that perfume again, even if 30 years have passed, our body and mind will react the same way they reacted back then. It would be as if it were happening now because in reality for our subconscious it is all happening in the present.

No matter how long ago the association was created, every time we experience something similar in the present time, our body will react according to what happened in the past. So, we could conclude that, actually, the past is not the past, but that the past is with us at all times.

Other associations that we store in the subconscious are those related to traumatic events we have lived through. Traumas are events that we were not able to process physically, mentally, and emotionally at the time they occurred. This causes the event to remain unfinished and pending in our mind.

If, for example, a person who was raped as a child could not process that terrible event, it is more than certain they will experience problems when having their first sexual and loving relationship. This is because their mind will immediately go back to the moment of the rape, making their body feel just as uncomfortable as it did then.

So, if when reacting to a certain situation, we react the same as when something similar happened to us, is what happened to us in the past, or is it with us in the present? If all that we have experienced is in the past, then why do we experience the symptoms or consequences now? The answer to these questions can only be found by concluding that, for the mind, the past does not exist.

The Soul and Time

In a previous chapter I explained the difference between spirit and soul, basically saying that the soul is an incarnated spirit. This spirit, this energy with its own consciousness and intelligence, would be the one that decides to incarnate a human body to experience and evolve through emotions. The soul, then, will face different situations in which it will learn both in love and in suffering, being this pain an amplifier of learning. It is to planet Earth that the spirits come to evolve in a way that they could not do in their ethereal form, through the emotions.

Just as there is no time for our subconscious, there is no time for the soul. What we call the subconscious, the soul does not see as limited to the existence of the physical body it is occupying, but it goes with it from life to life, from body to body, carrying all its memories with it in an unconscious way. This means that the subconscious is the result of the sum of memories and experiences that go with the soul from reincarnation to reincarnation.

Once again, we are faced with the task of explaining the inexplicable with the limited words of our language, in order to understand the characteristics of a disembodied entity, of a subtle energy with its own consciousness: the soul. I do not know if the word I should use to describe the part of the spirit that keeps the memories of another life should be subconscious, but I choose to use it because, in one way or another, this supposed subconscious of the spirit is fulfilling the same function.

If this is so, should we think that the subconscious is part of the soul and not of the mind? I will share a paragraph from the book *Workers of the Life Eternal*, psychographed by Chico Xavier, where Barceló, a spirit assistant who was destined to support the mentally ill disincarnated, who in turn was a teacher when he was in the physical plane, explains to André Luiz the importance of understanding that the information stored in our subconscious is not limited to the time of life in the physical body, but goes even further:

> *The subconscious is, in fact, the enlarged vault of our memories, a repository of emotions and desires, impulses and tendencies which are not projected onto the screen of immediate realizations, but which extend well beyond the limited realm of time in which a corporeal body moves. The subconscious represents the stratification of all the struggles resulting in mental and emotional acquisitions after the utilization of many bodies.*

This excerpt from Chico Xavier's work, along with texts I also read by Brian Weiss, Dolores Cannon, Michael Newton, Aurelio Mejia, and Jose Luis Cabouli only confirm this concept. Furthermore, since I started practicing hypnosis, I have come across stories in which it was clear that the past life events of those who came for a session were directly related to the symptoms they were experiencing in the current life. What's more, I could see that by them reliving those traumatic events from a supposed past, it made the symptom disappear immediately. Why? Because, without me being aware of it at the time, I was helping the soul to close a cycle, to complete what it had not been able to complete at the time, causing it to become entrapped.

Multisimultaneity

The word *simultaneity* refers to the relationship between two or more events occurring at the same time within a time frame of reference. So, if we use the word *multisimultaneity*, we are referring to multiple pairs of events happening at the same time within a time frame of reference. Confusing? Well, I will try to explain this idea in a better way in the following lines.

Having shared all the above concepts, we could ask ourselves the following question: if time is an illusion and everything happens now, if the past does not exist and it is with us now—in the form of symptoms—what would be the factors that affect our soul? Both the question and the explanation are complicated, but I will try to explain it in a simple way. First, I will share an example using linear time, past, present, and future, because this is what we understand more easily. Then, we will see it in quantum time. It is the same example I used in my book *Guiding Lost Souls*, but in this text I will explain it in a slightly different way.

Let's suppose John comes in for a consultation to try to understand the origin of his claustrophobia. During the session, he tells me about his first experience when he was a child and got into an elevator, where he suffered an anxiety attack feeling that he could not breathe and that he was going to die. John did not understand the cause of these symptoms, which continued to manifest throughout his life when he boarded planes, trains, or drove his car through tunnels.

We will use the following graph to show the supposed past lives John has had:

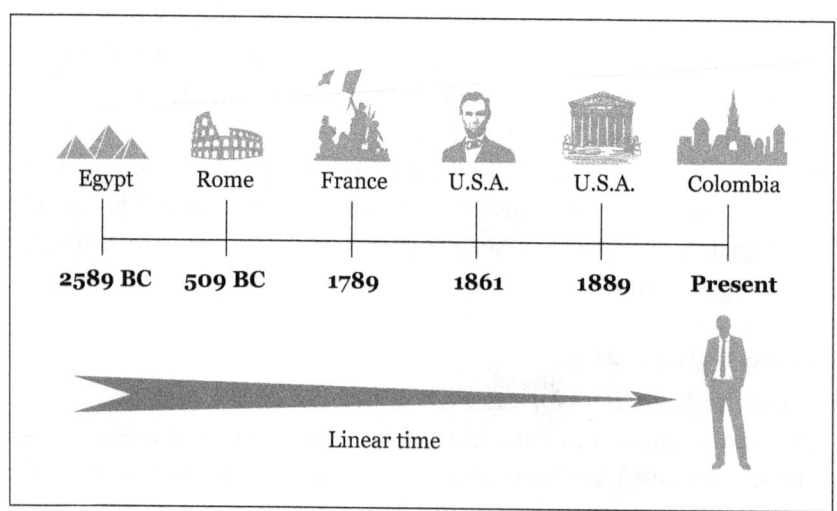

In the graph we can see that John had past lives in Egypt, Rome, France, the United States, and Colombia, where he currently resides. Let's continue to assume that, as we explore the symptoms, he visits the events in this life in which he experienced that suffocation and fear of dying. When I ask him to go back further to the first time he had those sensations—without using the expression *past life*—he goes back to one where he starts describing to me what he sees: pyramids and sphinxes. It is Egypt. As I continue to ask questions, he tells me that he is one of the servants of an important person and that he had just passed away. As I continue to ask him questions, John describes the ceremony that is taking place, in which they are putting the body in a kind of cave or burial chamber. John tells me about his difficulty breathing, the darkness of the place, and how the servants are asked to stand around the place where their master's body is lying.

He then tells me that the relatives come out and that suddenly he hears how the large stone that covered the entrance to the cave is moved to seal it with him and the other servants inside. Immediately, his body begins to stiffen, he feels the lack of air, the darkness, the fear of dying, and he tells me how, slowly, his body dies in fear and anguish.

If we were to analyze this event from the point of view of linear time, we would begin to make a series of erroneous assumptions. For example, we would refer to the life in Egypt as a past life, then assume that if John died of asphyxiation in Egypt, then he also experienced the same symptoms without understanding their origin in the following lives in Rome, France, the United States and Colombia. Why? Because these are the lives he lived after the one in Egypt. Going a little further and, following the structure of linear time, we would also think that there is nothing we can do to help him because "how would it be possible to help heal someone from something that happened in another body that no longer exists?" If we think that way, then, once that body is dead, the symptom should end in that life, it should stay in the past and would have no reason to affect him now. Do you understand all the mistakes we could make if we look at this event from the structure of linear time?

Now let's look at this same example from the point of view of quantum time, from the time understood by the soul in which everything happens now.

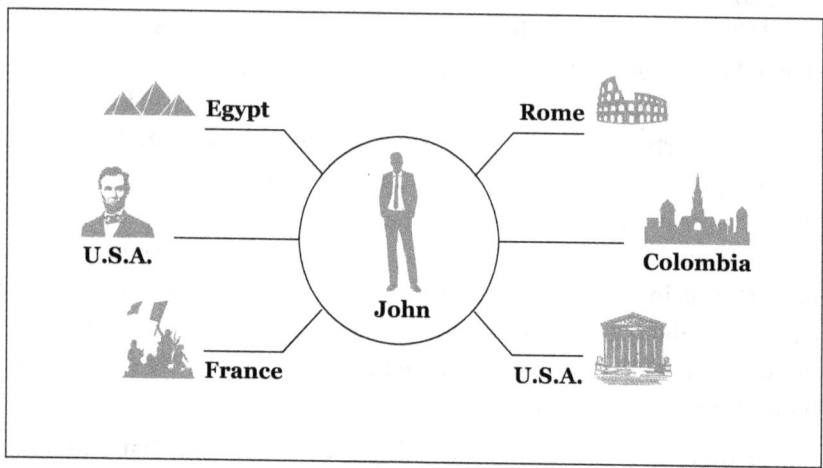

Looking at this new graphic, you can see that I have put all the lives that John has had around him. This would be the correct representation, because for John's soul everything is happening now. Let's look at this graphic as that of a computer network where the server, the main computer that stores and processes all the data, is at the center and the workstations, the terminals or computers, are around it in a star-like arrangement. The server is the one that interconnects the other computers, and these at the same time connect to the server to obtain information. From this point of view, everything that happens on the computers and workstations affects the server, and everything that affects the server affects the computers.

Now, let's imagine that a computer, one of the terminals, is infected by a virus, and neither the computers nor the server has antivirus software. What would happen under this assumption? Well, when the computer is infected, it will infect the server connected to it and, at the same time, the server will infect the other computers which are connected to it. This is what actually happens with what we call past lives and with our soul.

Now, let's replace the server with John's soul and the computers connected to it with John's supposed past lives. Once this is done, we can understand that, for John's soul, everything is happening now, that the past lives are not really past and that whatever has happened or is still happening in them will have repercussions in his current life. Now, let's replace the virus that infected one of the computers with the traumatic death he had in Egypt where he died locked up and suffocated. This, by logic, is going to affect John's soul and, if not addressed therapeutically in this life, will most likely damage a future one as well.

Following this line, let's imagine now that a computer technician is hired to install an antivirus program on the server. The antivirus software will sweep all the stations connected to it, eliminating any trace of the virus. Now, to understand this better, let's replace the computer technician with the therapist and the antivirus program with the understanding of what happened in John's life in Egypt and the ability to complete and close that experience forever. John's soul will do a sweep of all the events similar to that death and eliminate the emotions and symptoms related to those events.

Up to this point we have used an example in which the soul is being affected by an event in a past life. This would clearly explain the concept of simultaneity, but what actually happens is that our soul carries traumas from several lives, not just one. So, let's suppose that John died in his life in Rome in the Roman coliseum, being a Christian who was attacked by a lion. Let's also add that, in his life in France, he died from a sword wound that went through his back, and that in one of his lives in the United States, he died from a bullet wound in the Civil War. If we see how many traumatic deaths John has had in his past lives, we could deduce that all of those traumas are with him now in this body at the same time. This would be the concept of multisimultaneity.

While we have only used traumatic deaths with the supposed causes of those deaths, we must remember that the symptoms (physical, emotional, or mental) that manifest in our current life are not only associated with physical traumas, but also with other types of events in past lives including those from childhood, intrauterine life, our time in the womb, and even after the death of the physical body in a past life. Later I will explain all of this under the concept of soul entrapment.

The Soul, Trauma, and Time

The word *trauma* comes from the Greek *τραũμαy* and means wound. This word refers to a physical injury by an external agent or from an emotional shock that generates persistent damage in the unconscious. To continue with the context of this book, we will focus on trauma of the psychological type because this is not only associated with the mind, but also with the soul.

By psychological trauma, we mean the emotional shock that generates a mental imbalance. This trauma is caused by an intense fear or by not being able to control a real or potential danger. It can occur when a person is in the role of observer or when they are victims of these situations of terror.

What I have noticed through the practice of hypnosis is that most of the traumas that people bring to the session, although many times they do not remember it, originated in childhood and even before their birth while they were in the womb. The explanation is that our childhood is the stage in which we are most vulnerable to what happens around us and the stage in which we are usually simple observers of everything that happens without having a good understanding or being able to control these situations.

All the traumatic events we experience at an early age are recorded in our subconscious mind almost immediately and remain there indefinitely, since our critical mind is not yet developed. In addition, during the first six years of life, the child's mind is in an alpha state, an expanded state of consciousness that allows it to learn and process everything more quickly.

As an example, we can mention those children who grew up watching their parents argue constantly, or who witnessed the physical and emotional abuse to which their mother was subjected by their father, as well as those who lived in homes where their parents were addicted to alcohol or drugs. In short, the list could be endless, but in these cases our mind is affected, causing an imbalance. Other events that cause trauma and imbalance could be rape, molestation, accidents, and the death of loved ones.

The subconscious is nothing more than the set of experiences, traumas, and emotions of the soul that go with it from body to body. Under this premise and the premise that the soul does not understand time, I can affirm that traumas do not understand time either. That is to say, that these traumas are carried by the soul to other lives, other bodies.

Does this mean that from the moment we are born we already have the trauma? When we talk about being born again, we are really talking about reincarnation, the process by which the soul is enveloped in a corporeal shell. For the soul, there is only one life with experiences in different bodies. This means that the soul, when reincarnating, already brings the trauma with it and that this will manifest itself in the form of symptoms (physical, emotional, or mental), when it goes through a situation or emotion similar to the one it experienced when that trauma was engraved in its subconscious.

It is worth mentioning that when the conscious mind knows that this traumatic event is going to overload you in the present life, that is, that it is too much to be processed at that moment, it removes it, encapsulates it, and sends it to the subconscious mind. This means that, consciously, we do not remember what happened, but that when we experience something similar, we react in the same way without understanding why. So how do we differentiate between past life traumas and current life traumas? I think this would be very difficult to determine starting from the premise that the soul does not understand past, present, and future times. Let's remember that, when we reincarnate, we go through a kind of spiritual amnesia that does not allow us to remember our past lives, although in reality those traumatic experiences are stored in our subconscious. Because of this great detail, when people are in a state of hypnotic trance, they return to the traumatic events that they had completely suppressed from their mind.

So, I dare to say that it does not matter if a trauma took place in a past life or in a current life, it goes with the soul, and it is affecting the soul now. Therefore, it is fundamental to handle the concept of quantum time while accompanying people in hypnotic trance. For both the patient and the therapist, the trauma is originating symptoms now, and it is in the now that we must work with it to eliminate the ailments.

THE PURPOSE OF THE SOUL

Remembering that the soul is in reality an incarnated spirit, it is necessary to begin this chapter by understanding what the purpose of the spirit is. What better explanation can there be than that given by the spirits themselves in Allan Kardec's *The Spirits' Book*.

In questions 114 and 115, they explain that spirits are created neither good nor bad, but that they follow a process by which they evolve and, upon achieving this, pass from a lower to a higher order. They go on to say that God created all spirits simple and ignorant, giving each one a mission with the sole objective of enlightening them and progressively reaching perfection through knowledge and truth. Here, the key word would be 'progressively' because I understand this as the lives we will have to live in search of that perfection.

Something interesting the spirits relate in this book is regarding the knowledge that the spirit acquires while undergoing the trials that God imposes on them. Those who accept their mission reach the goal faster, and those who do not, suffer with displeasure because of it, far from the promised perfection and bliss.

To give us a better understanding, we are asked to see spirits as inexperienced children who acquire little by little the knowledge they lack, going through the different stages of life. If the child is rebellious, it will remain ignorant and imperfect.

115. Have some spirits been created good and others evil?
"God has created all spirits simple and ignorant, i.e., without knowledge. God has given each of them a mission. It is aimed at enlightening them and progressively leading them toward perfection through knowledge of the truth in order to draw them near to God. In that perfection, they will find eternal bliss without any troubles. Spirits acquire knowledge by experiencing the trials that God has imposed on them. Some humbly accept these trials and thus arrive more quickly at their destiny, whereas others cannot endure them without complaining; thus, through their own fault these latter ones remain far from the perfection and bliss promised to them."
– Then are all spirits at their origin, ignorant and inexperienced like children, who gradually acquire the knowledge they lack by passing through the different phases of human life?
"Yes, that is an accurate comparison. How much children improve depends on their behavior – rebellious children remain ignorant and imperfect. However, human life has an ending, whereas that of spirits extends to infinity."

So, how is it that God assigns trials to spirits? How is it that they progressively reach perfection by acquiring knowledge? What do they mean by missions that, when not accepted, cause suffering? To understand how the spirit advances in its progressive evolution through the trials it faces, we would have to talk about reincarnation. And, if we are going to talk about reincarnation, then we would have to begin by understanding what is the organization, so to speak, of the spirit world, of the place from which these spirits come.

There is quite a bit of literature that refers to this information. One of the most comprehensive sources is *Many Lives, Many Masters* by Brian Weiss. On the other hand, Michael Newton, in his books *The Destiny of Souls* and *Life Between Lives*, explains how the map of the spiritual world is composed and what supposedly happens during the time that the spirit returns to it after the death of its physical body and the time before returning (reincarnating). I think it would be absurd to repeat what is mentioned in these books without having corroborated or confirmed these concepts through my own hypnosis sessions.

Taking the definitions that I have also shared in my book *The Purpose of My Soul*, we can get an idea of the process that a spirit goes through before and after reincarnating. We will also get to know everything that will affect us once we are reincarnated: lessons learned, karma, contracts, choice of body, among other events. Many times, these will make us feel like victims and, by not understanding them, will also contribute to the fact that these situations can become traumatic events that can result in the entrapment of our soul.

Below, I will share some of these definitions.

Spirit Groups

Spirit groups are a group of spirits with a common interest and who are basically at the same level of evolution. Understand this group as classmates in a school classroom who will undertake together their learning path, sharing experiences, living happy and sad moments, facing challenges, missions and helping each other evolve.

The spiritual group is constituted from the moment the spirit is created as such. Some will be able to advance more than others and will become part of new groups; others will take a little longer in their evolution, having to repeat the lessons, just as it happens in school.

The interesting thing about spiritual groups is that almost always the color of their energy is the same, as well as what motivates them to be part of that group. It has also been noted that the level of spiritual evolution is almost the same among all members. The color of the energy is the one that allows to identify the evolutionary level of the spirit. The colors start from white, then yellow, continuing in combinations of pink, orange, to darker colors such as purple, which can mean a more evolved spirit.

In my book *My Soul's Purpose*, I relate my experience with Dodris, a spirit guide who manifested through a colleague in a hypnotic trance and whose color was purple. Coincidentally, it was the color of his energy that let me know the type of spirit we were communicating with.

The members of a spirit group usually reincarnate together, but not in every reincarnation. Each member plays a different role in their reincarnation, which not only allows them to learn, experience, and evolve, but also helps other members of the group who are incarnated to evolve through this learning.

We could say, then, that the members of a spirit group decide to take roles in the reincarnations, just as artists would do in a play. The big difference in this case is that this play would be made according to our needs, according to the trials and lessons that we must face in it in order to achieve our evolution.

More than once I have witnessed the joy of my clients when they meet again with the members of their group during a hypnotic trance. Several have mentioned the names and roles they play in their current reincarnation and others have spoken about those spirits they consider their soul mates, with whom they frequently reincarnate. Through their descriptions I have been able to appreciate the great companionship and love that exists between them and the recognition of the role that each one plays in their spiritual evolution.

It is worth mentioning that, as Michael Newton says, it seems that the spirits that play the role of our parents are not part of our spiritual group, but of others with whom we interact and agree to reincarnate. From them we can learn from both love and suffering, the latter being an amplifier of that learning. Michael Newton goes even further, stating that, with these other groups to which the spirits of our parents belong, the interaction is to work on issues related to karma. This is something that I have not been able to prove, but I have corroborated that most of the traumas we carry with us were generated during childhood, many times as a consequence of what we experienced through our parents while we were in a vulnerable situation due to our physical and mental immaturity. I do not know if this could be called karma, but these experiences definitely mark us for life and compel us to evolve spiritually.

I have also noticed that karma (the action of paying off a debt) makes us feel like victims of others, when, in reality, we are only feeling what we made others feel. Later I will explain about the roles we play in our reincarnations, but for now it is necessary to understand that every victim has been a perpetrator before, which means that they are paying karma. It is this role of victim that makes us enter into a spiral of self-sabotage if we do not accept what we have had to live, seeing it as part of our spiritual evolution.

I remember the case of a patient who had been a victim of molestation during her childhood and adolescence, for which she had suffered a great deal. In a hypnotic state, she returned to a life in which she was a soldier who broke into houses and raped women. In this life, she was feeling in her own flesh what in her life as a soldier she had made those women feel.

The Guides

Spirit guides are spirits with a more advanced level of spiritual evolution, in charge of guiding, as their name implies, spirits that form a spirit group. Understand that in this organization of groups and guides, there is no chain of command. They are there to help us continue our spiritual evolution.

How do these guides help us to evolve? To better understand this concept, let us think of the work of a mentor to whom we turn for guidance toward the goals we wish to achieve. The mentor will not tell us what to do, nor will he give us orders, nor will he impose his way of thinking on us. The mentor will be close by to guide us, to suggest certain actions to take, based on his or her experience. It will be up to us whether we follow those suggestions or not. In the end, we are the ones responsible for our learning, exercising our free will at all times.

A spiritual guide:
- Will never give us orders.
- Will never make predictions.
- Will not impose itself on our spiritual evolution.
- Will never tell us exactly what to do.
- Will speak little, but say a lot.

Our spirit guide will help us evaluate the lessons we ourselves planned before reincarnating and examine the goals achieved at the end of each incarnation. It is our spirit guide who usually greets us at the portal (the entrance to the spirit world) each time we return to this place.

In reality, we are never alone, neither when we are in the spiritual world, nor while we are incarnated. Our guide (or guides) will always be there to assist us when we ask for it. Many of my clients, during the hypnotic trance state, have mentioned seeing a bright light coming to them to communicate something, either during the time they were in my office or after death in a past life. "It is my guide. He is always with me," is what many have commented at such times.

People who experienced such communication with their guides during their hypnosis session were quick to describe the infinite love that this being of light conveyed to them, as well as the feeling of not being judged by them, no matter what they had done in the incarnation that had just ended. "Everything is learning. Don't be so hard on yourself," is usually the message the guides convey to us upon receiving us.

On the other hand, a misconception that some people who attend a spiritual hypnosis session have is to believe that, being in a trance, they will be able to establish a communication with their guide at will so they can tell them what to do about the situation they are going through. Many expect their spiritual guide to solve their 'problem' without realizing that the circumstance is in reality a lesson they must overcome in order to continue evolving. It would be like asking our teacher to give us the answers to an exam.

On some occasions, patients, when communicating with their guides, have felt a kind of blockage on their part. That is, they were not allowed to access certain information because it would ruin the lesson they were going through at that moment. Our guide is not there to solve our problems, but to help us evolve.

The "Council" of the Elders

Also called the council of the Wise, this is a group of more advanced spirits whose function is to evaluate the progress of spirits returning to the spirit world after the end of their incarnation. My clients have described this place in different ways. Some describe it as an open environment, like an amphitheater of sorts; others describe it as an enclosed place with high ceilings and columns.

The council helps the spirits assess the overall progress of their evolution. While it is true that communication appears to be direct with them, many have reported that their spirit guide was at their side or behind them as they interacted with these wiser spirits.

The description given by both Michael Newton's clients and mine is that of standing in front of a long table, where the wise spirits are seated side by side. Common details in the stories include the color of their energy—which can be darker, showing greater evolution—and the use of different colored robes and a kind of medallion on the chest.

The Elders not only help us evaluate our past lives and evolution in general, but also provide us with complementary guidance to that of our guides.

The Library

Remember that people in trance who return to these places in the spiritual world describe them with the vocabulary they possess in the present incarnation. Some have portrayed this area as a space with many shelves filled with books; others have referred to it as an open place with various crystals. What is found within the library is the past life information of all spirits. Some have used the name akashic records, which would be a kind of logbook.

To this place, we spirits return to study our lives, to evaluate them in order to have a better understanding of the lessons we have learned, those we have yet to cultivate, and those we have been trying to internalize for a few lifetimes. While it is true that some have reported going to this place alone, most have reported going to the library with their guide, who helps them evaluate the last incarnation shortly after they have disincarnated, after they have returned to the spiritual world.

One thing that has happened a few times is that upon opening these books they are empty, causing great confusion to the spirit trying to appreciate their evolution. When I asked them to ask their guide why the pages were blank, the answer was, "You must want to see in order to understand." They had to be ready to face what they were about to see. But why should we be ready to see what is on those pages? When they open the books, they describe seeing images or videos that they can interact with as if it were virtual reality. There, they can see both what they did and what other people felt as a result of their actions. This moment would be a challenge for us, taking responsibility for our actions.

Karma

Often confused with a punishment, the word *karma* (in Sanskrit) is the energy that is generated from the acts of a human being. Karma is understood as the law of cause and effect, the law of balance, of equilibrium.

From the point of view of spirituality and reincarnation, this means that we will experience in our own flesh whatever we make someone else experience. It is for this reason that, personally, I do not believe that there are good or bad spirits, but only spirits that are more evolved than others. When someone does something 'bad' from the human being's point of view, they are not really doing it because they are bad, but out of ignorance. If they knew that what they are causing in others, they will have to feel themselves later on, they would not do it.

Countless times I have facilitated sessions for people who were abused or raped in this life, experiencing all kinds of symptoms and setbacks as a result of it and submerged in a victim role, who upon returning to a past life were able to see what originated their current situation. To their surprise, both men and women, they were the violators in their past life. Upon reincarnation, they realized that they now had to face the consequence of what they had done in another body.

I would say that the concept of karma is one of the most difficult to understand for those who are trapped in the role of victim. Understanding what karma is entails not only understanding that many of the situations we are living in may be the product of our own actions—both in this life and in a previous one—but it also entails taking responsibility for those actions, whether we like it or not.

Knowing how karma works, and how this law of cause and effect works, teaches us to consider the feelings of others and to put ourselves in the other person's shoes. For example, if I think about being unfaithful to my partner, karma teaches me to put myself in the scenario of that partner being unfaithful to me. Then, the decision about my actions will be based on putting myself in the other person's shoes first.

Karma, then, becomes an important point when planning our next reincarnation, since apart from the lessons we program for our evolution, we will also have to consider the debts we have acquired with others.

Contracts

These would be the agreements we make with other spirits, both of our spiritual group and those of another group, to interact once we are reincarnated. The purpose of this interaction is diverse. One can interact to learn a lesson, to settle karma, to heal relationships between parents, children, siblings, partners, and so on.

As with the concept of karma, the concept of contracts can also be somewhat difficult to process. If for example during childhood we have suffered all kinds of mistreatment and abuse from our parents and as a consequence of these, we are immersed in great depression and experience psychological symptoms, would it be easy to understand and accept that we ourselves chose those parents? Would it be easy for us to accept that we ourselves chose those situations of suffering?

Most will say that this does not make sense, for why would our soul plan to suffer during childhood, when we cannot even defend ourselves. It is difficult to explain from an earthly point of view why this works this way. Many of my clients have reported interacting with the spirit of their parents before they were born. It would be during this interaction that they would agree to play the role of parent and child (the contract). This evidence can also be found in the books of Michael Newton and Dolores Cannon.

I still remember the session of Luz, who had come to Charlotte, North Carolina to have a session with my teacher Aurelio Mejia, and in which I was able to participate as well. Luz's great sadness was due to the fact that her mother had abandoned her with her grandmother when she was only five. Luz, who at the time of the session had a young daughter, could not understand how her mother could have made such a decision. While Luz was in a deep trance, I asked Aurelio for authorization to take control of the session. I asked the patient to go back to the moment when she was planning the reincarnation she was going to have as Luz. As she listed the lessons to be learned, she said that at the age of five her mother was going to leave her. I asked her if she was choosing that lesson, and she said yes, that her spirit had to experience that in order to learn to be independent.

When Luz came out of the hypnotic trance, she did not remember anything she had said during the session. That day, Luz went from feeling like a victim to taking control of her life, understanding that many of the circumstances she had gone through in her life had been planned by herself before she was born.

I have encountered many other cases like Luz's. Even if it does not make sense to us, we should always keep this in mind. When we go through difficult moments, we should consider that it seems more than likely that our spirit planned that experience in order to learn, even more so, if that painful situation is related to someone else, such as our parents, children, partners, etc.

The Lessons

One of the most controversial and difficult-to-understand concepts is the one that says the soul chooses the lessons to learn in its next reincarnation. It will choose different situations and interactions with other souls for that purpose. It may sound unbelievable even to the therapist, especially when we are talking about rape, child abuse, and tragic accidents. Why would a spirit need to learn through suffering? The answer can be complex. It could be karma, an acquired debt, or it could be what I have heard so many times in session, "I had to learn to forgive with love and without judgment."

The situations are innumerable in reality, but we could also add tragic accidents (which are not really accidents) or the death or loss of a child, among other tragedies. We choose these circumstances based on what we believe our spirit needs to learn in order to continue evolving, but what we don't really know is how we will react to these situations. Some extreme and painful ones may generate a trauma that ends up causing the entrapment of our soul.

These experiences appear without exception in hypnosis sessions, and it is the same people who, in hypnotic trance, realize that they were the ones who chose them. It is like a road map to follow with different goals to achieve in each life. These lessons are planned with the help of our guides and our spirit group. When a lesson is learned, the spirit plans the next list of goals and thus continues to evolve with a sort of tailored roadmap.

The challenge comes when a lesson is not learned. This can happen for different reasons: feeling like a victim, not taking ownership of the lesson in front of us, running away from painful lessons, or not wanting to forgive, among others.

When a lesson is not learned, while we are incarnated, it will come back to us again and again disguised as another person or situation. This can be clearly seen in our lives when the same pattern manifests. How many times have we seen people enter into a relationship with the same type of abusive person time and time again; still others who are constantly hurt by hurtful expressions that affect their self-esteem, having started with their parents since childhood.

What I have noticed in the hypnosis sessions I have facilitated, and this is also mentioned by Robert Schwartz in his book *Your Soul's Plan*, is that from the beginning of our life we experience the opposite of what we are supposed to learn. If what I experienced was lovelessness, then it is more than certain that what I will have to learn is to give and receive love. If what we experienced was emotional abuse that hurt our self-esteem, then we may need to learn about self-love and how to love ourselves.

The most common questions my clients bring to their hypnosis session is, "What do I need to learn?" and "Why does this always happen to me?" If we try to understand the lessons from the point of view of spirituality, that is, taking into account that we are a spirit having a human experience, and that this planet is but one of the many schools that the universe has and to which we go to learn for our evolution, we would know that we do not need a hypnosis session to remember or decipher what we need to learn. We only need to be aware of the pattern that is present in our life, those very similar situations that we have faced over time, to realize that what we have to learn is the opposite of what we have been experiencing.

Later on, we will see that those lessons which are presented to us again and again may have their origin in a past life. They may be the result of an event in another life that is causing us to sabotage ourselves in the current one.

What types of lessons do we plan for before we reincarnate? The lessons are endless, but there are a few that are more difficult to learn: forgiveness, love, self-esteem, physical and emotional limitations, being one—that is, that we are all connected and come from the same source—and so on.

I remember the conversation I had with a friend who was worried about her son's behavior. I was trying to explain to her how it is that we, before we are born, choose the lessons we will have during our lifetime, and I expressed my opinion that she and her son might have something to work on and learn together, having agreed on this reincarnation. I wanted her to see that what she considered a problem was an opportunity to learn, either in love or in suffering. However, her response indicated to me how complicated it was for her to understand that concept: "If we have planned everything before we were born, then why make an effort or study? If everything is already predestined, what does it matter what we do if the outcome is already predefined?"

As we plan the challenges we will go through on Earth with the goal of learning, there is no guarantee that we will actually learn from them when we reincarnate. There is no telling how we will react or deal with them at that time, as there are so many variables that come into play.

Think of a lesson we might have planned in the spiritual world and the circumstance we will face in order to learn it. Now, let's visualize this lesson and that circumstance as a question that has multiple possible answers to choose from, such as we used to find in school exams. But imagine that those possible answers do not go from A to E, but from A to infinity, and that there is no one hundred percent correct answer, as they are all valid. Such are the lessons we plan. It does not matter how we are going to face them or how we are going to react to them, because there will always be something to learn. While it is true that there may be an answer that will give us a higher score, the other answers we choose will also contribute to the final result.

On the other hand, an equally relevant aspect is the choice of the place where we will be born. If we see planet Earth as a university, let's think of countries, continents, or territories as faculties with different specialties. Depending on the country where we are born, we will be exposed to different societies, cultures, laws, and religions. It is not the same to be born and grow up in Switzerland, for example, as in India. Each country and each culture will offer us a different challenge from an economic, cultural, and belief point of view. Similarly, it will not be the same to be reincarnated as a woman, for example, in more liberal countries than in others where the female gender is strongly repressed by culture and religion. Each territory will allow us to learn something different and evolve in different ways.

There are places that are constantly at war, exposing their inhabitants to bombings, deaths, destruction, and living in a state of constant anxiety. There are other countries exposed to natural disasters (earthquakes, tsunamis, hurricanes, or floods). As absurd as it may sound, living in these countries allows its residents to obtain specialized training.

The Choice of the Body

One of the most important steps in the preparation of the lessons is the choice of the body. Each test will require a certain body, from a female to a male. If, for example, the spirit seeks to learn about unconditional love, perhaps the body it chooses will be female in order to experience the love of becoming a mother. If it needs to experience and overcome limitations, it may choose a body with a disability, either from birth or as a result of an accident.

This is why, when we see a person with a genetic disability, we should ask ourselves the following question: Does that person have this condition because they were born into that family or were they born into that family in order to have that condition? On the other hand, regarding accidents that have left some physical impairment, we could ask ourselves these questions: How could that spirit learn what limitation is without first having experienced what it is like to have no limitation at all? Are accidents really accidents?

More than once I have had to facilitate sessions in which the patient in trance gets the answer to what the accident is for, rather than why. Although it is difficult to believe and understand, there are spirits who, once incarnated, unconsciously attract accidents as a kind of escape from various lessons that they have to face, that is, to avoid going through this or that lesson.

How can this be possible? To begin with, let's remember that we have free will and we ourselves can attract to our lives different situations that will either help us or end up blocking us. Then, under this premise, we can, unconsciously, generate circumstances that make us not to pass this or that lesson that we came to learn, causing a delay in our evolution, because sooner or later we will have to pass it anyway.

During my hypnosis sessions, when using Michael Newton's Life Between Lives technique, I have listened to my clients in hypnotic trance explain the various reasons that led them to choose the body they had in their current reincarnation. "I am choosing a body that is overweight and not very beautiful so that, in this life, I can avoid any distractions and focus on what I need to learn."

In the book *The Messengers* by Chico Xavier, we find the following description of the human body that Aniceto, a fellow servant, gives to André Luiz:

> *You can now identify the movements of living matter. Each organ is an autonomous department in the cellular realm, but subordinate to the individual's thoughts. Each gland is a center of active service. There is a great similarity between the human body and the modern machine. They both run on fuel, but with the difference that in humans, chemical combustion obeys the spiritual sense that directs organic life. Our mind doesn't process merely our character, reason, memory, direction, balance and understanding.*

It is in this way, then, we can understand the human body as our own universe within the universe in which we live. Each body we occupy brings its own challenges and constraints. The body we choose will cause us to experience the circumstances we plan in order to learn our lessons.

What other reasons might a spirit have for choosing a body with physical limitations? Based on my studies and books I have read, but especially what I have found in the hypnosis sessions I have facilitated, I can say that a spirit may also prefer a condition or limitation to help their close environment learn and evolve. More than once I have had relatives of children with Down Syndrome, and what could be learned from them? Among the many teachings it brings us are unconditional love, compassion, patience, and non-judgment.

I still remember what happened in the session of Luz, of whom I spoke above and whose mother had disappeared from her life when she was five years old. Using the Role Change technique, the hypnotherapist Aurelio Mejia began to talk, through her, with the spirit of Luz's brother, who had a mental condition that made him process everything in a slower way. When asked why he had chosen that condition in this life and what he had to learn, he answered: "Love. There are no barriers. I understand more than you. I am not limited. In this world, people think we are different, but we are not. I could have gone somewhere else, but I wanted to be here with you so you can learn that there are no limits in life, that I can and you can. I love you sister."

Spiritual Amnesia

After carefully selecting the lessons of our next life with the help of our guides and members of our spiritual group, always taking into account the contracts (the choice of parents, partners, children, among others) and the karma we will have to pay, and after even choosing the body that we will adopt and that will serve us to achieve our goals, some might think that everything is ready to be born on Earth, but it is not so. When we arrive here, we will be exposed to what I call spiritual amnesia, that is, to forget who we are and what we came here for.

This is the greatest challenge we will face as it can put all our plans at risk. The incarnated spirit remembers nothing of what it planned in the spirit world, including with whom it will interact. Spiritual amnesia turns human life into a real ordeal, but one that ultimately exists for our own benefit. How so? Well, let's imagine that two enemies in a past life were involved in a fight in which one of them ended up dead at the hands of the other who was involved in feelings of revenge and hatred. Since killing acquires karma, let's say that in the next reincarnation these spirits are sent this time as father and son, forced to be together and learn hand in hand about love and forgiveness.

If we were not exposed to spiritual amnesia, can you imagine what the father's reaction would be like when he sees that his son who has just been born was his enemy in the last life? What would the relationship between them be like? Remembering can alter what we have come to learn. In this case, remembering would ruin the opportunity for both spirits to learn about love and forgiveness.

One thing I have noticed over the years of practice is that, in general, children have the ability to remember past life events and even to see spirits. But as they grow older, these memories disappear and their sensitivity to see energies is blocked by few, either by fear, ignorance of parents on the subject, society, or religion. Nowadays, thanks to the Internet, you can find many documented cases of children who remember their past lives. They mention the place where they lived, their relatives, their profession, and even in some cases how they died or who had killed them.

Michael Newton explains how his patients, while in a hypnotic trance in the spirit world, claimed to recognize who their partner would be when they were reincarnated. This would be a contingency mechanism to ensure that both reincarnated spirits would begin an interaction to carry out the lessons they had come to learn together. Some had chosen to recognize each other by looking into each other's eyes, others by smiling. I was able to verify this in my own sessions, when my patients talked to me about identifying themselves by voice or eyes. I still remember when, years after we were married, my wife Catherine told me that when she met me, she knew she had to marry me. She didn't say 'I felt' or 'I wanted,' she said 'I had to.' For my part, as I looked into her eyes, I felt like I had known her forever. Undoubtedly, our spirits recognized each other at that moment to set our learning plan in motion.

***

So far, we have seen some of the components of the spiritual world and reincarnation, the steps we follow or tools we use to learn and evolve. Referring to what I mentioned at the beginning of the chapter, in *The Spirits' Book* by Allan Kardec, we find this idea:

> "God has created all spirits simple and ignorant, i.e., without knowledge. God has given each of them a mission. It is aimed at enlightening them and progressively leading them toward perfection through knowledge of the truth in order to draw them near to God."

Thus, we (the spirits) are achieving perfection in this school called planet Earth, planning lessons and tests helped by our spirit guides and supported by our spirit group, experiencing the emotions that we can only live here while we are incarnated, while trying to remember that we are all one and that the secret of life lies in unconditional love and forgiveness. All this happens while we are in spiritual amnesia, in a world of confusion as we try to reconstruct who we are and what we are here for, while we learn to use our heart as a GPS to reach our destination and goal.

The Hunter

Chris' case is hard to forget. He came to me after Jon, his father, had a hypnosis session facilitated by me. Among the things his dad had wanted to work on was concern about Chris' situation, who after an accident had lost the ability to continue playing baseball professionally. For the family, it had been a very sad event.

During his session and after visiting a past life, Jon came to a place he described as a sort of library with several high shelves and drawers. He described to me that he could float to those shelves and open those drawers, which contained cards. As I asked him for more information, he told me that they contained records of different people's lives. As he got to Chris' card, he could see that in a past life he had been happy exploring, but was killed by Indians. "He was happy, and they took that away from him," he reported.

When asked how that scene related to Chris' current life, he told me it was the same thing. He was happy and he was exploring, referring to the sport he played. People told him he was good and he was forced to keep playing. They had taken his happiness away from him. Chris wanted to do something else, but for the sake of making others happy, he had agreed to play baseball. This had been a revelation to Jon, as he didn't know his son felt this way.

A few days later I received a call from Chris to schedule his own hypnosis session. When he introduced himself, he told me that he was Jon's son and that upon watching the video of his father's session, he had been shocked at the information his father had gained. "My father said things that I had never told him," he relayed to me.

When he came to his session, he expressed that he wanted to work on two symptoms that continually bothered him. One was a great sadness that would come over him from time to time for no reason. He told me that he went through periods when he felt empty and sad without knowing why. The other was the injury he had suffered in his knee while practicing baseball when he had a promising future. In the search for the source of his sadness, we come to the past life that I will share below. In his past life we also find the real reason why he would have suffered that accident in this life.

Antonio: Now that you are there, I want you to look at your feet and tell me what you are wearing.

Chris: Nothing.

A: Now, feel your body. Does it feel male or female?

C: Male.

A: Young or old?

C: Middle-aged.

A: What are you wearing?

C: I have a shirt and something covering my private parts.

A: Now, I want you to see your skin. What color is it?

C: Very tanned.

A: Are you wearing any ornaments on your arms or head?

C: I have bracelets.

A: Is your hair short or long?

C: It's long. I feel very upset and fierce.

A: Why do you feel fierce?

C: I feel dominant. I'm holding a spear.

A: Look around you, what do you see?

C: Jungle.

A: Are there others near you?

C: No. I live in a kind of mud hut.

A: Go into that hut and see if there is anyone there.

C: Yes, there is a woman. She is my wife. I feel that others are afraid of me.

Chris had come to a past life where he was sort of an Indian. I could tell that everything he was describing to me was a tiny percentage compared to what he was experiencing. I could see his eyes, which, though closed, moved from side to side as if scanning the activity of the scene.

C: My wife is tall. She has tanned skin. She is wearing something to cover her breasts and private parts. She has a necklace. I think I was hunting.

A: Do you have children?

C: No. I feel that there are other people near my hut.

A: Ask them why they are afraid of you.

C: They say I am bad-tempered and mean.

A: Look inside your heart. What is it that makes you bad-tempered? Why are you so upset?

C: I have to do everything myself. Hunting. Nobody does it right, so I have to do it myself. I do it anyway because it has to be done.

A: How many are in your group?

C: About ten people.

A: And do you feel responsible for everyone else?

C: Yes.

I asked Chris to step away from that scene and go to another significant moment in that man's life. His eyes began to move from side to side, as if watching a movie and looking for the information I had asked him for.

A: Three, two, one. There you are.

C: I'm very happy. I have a daughter. She is a little girl, and I am very protective of her.

A: How is your wife?

C: She is fine. We are very happy. I'm not upset anymore.

A: What has changed?

C: My daughter. She has brown eyes, they look very familiar, it's Louis! he said excitedly, referring to his sister in this life.

A: Now, that you are happy and have reconnected with your daughter, I want you to walk away from that scene and go to the next important event in that man's life. Three, two, one. You're already there.

C: "I'm sad," she commented mournfully and tearfully. "They're gone."

A: Who is gone?

C: My wife and my daughter. They took them away.

A: Who took them?

C: Some people in shining armor.

A: And where were you when they took them?

C: Hunting. I am very sad.

A: What about the others in your group?

C: Everyone is sad. They took a lot of people away. I don't want to be here.

A: Have you seen the men in armor before?

C: No.

A: Had you heard of them?

C: No.

A: What do you plan to do now?

C: Nothing [he answered with a resigned face].

A: Let's get away from this scene. Let's go to the next key event in this man's life. Three, two, one. You're already there.

C: I'm old and I'm in a garden. I don't hunt anymore. Like from the garden, which is very green. I feel empty.

A: Because you miss your wife and daughter.

C: Yes.

A: Do you feel any pain?

C: My legs.

A: What about them?

C: They hurt from hunting so much.

A: I want you to move to the moment when that body dies and your spirit comes out of it. What do you think you had to learn in that life?

C: Not to give up, not to hate.

A: Did you pass that lesson?

C: Yes.

A: Chris says that in his life he feels sad from time to time for no apparent reason in his current life. Is that sadness he feels related in any way to this life you just lived?

C: Yes.

A: How is it related?

C: It was taken away from him.

A: You mean your wife and daughter?

C: Happiness.

A: So, every time he feels something is taken away, he reacts the same way?

C: Yes.

Chris had recognized his daughter from that life as his sister in the current life when I asked him to look into her eyes. That's why I asked him the following question:

A: You were sad that your wife and daughter had been taken away from you, but did you realize that you have gotten your daughter back in this life, who is now your sister Louis?

C: Yes [he answered, smiling].

A: Then you have nothing to be sad about.

C: I'm so happy! [he said, crying with emotion].

A: Then, put a lot of joy in your heart because you have your daughter back as your sister, so you have a very special connection with her.

That was how Chris had gone to the origin of the sadness he felt. His soul had been trapped in the hunter's past life. Realizing that his daughter in that life had returned as his sister made him feel that there was no longer any reason to be sad. His soul had been freed from the entrapment in which it had been trapped.

The Conquistador

As I continued to talk to his spirit, that aspect of Chris that is connected to the spirit world at all times and supposedly has more information,

I asked him if the pain in his legs that the hunter felt was related to the pain in his legs that he feels in the current life. He replied that it was not. Then, I asked him to continue floating upward. He told me that he saw several lights in the distance, but there was one main one. What he was seeing were spirits. I suggested that he ask that spirit to identify himself. When he did, the word leg came to his mind.

Chris: I see someone.

Antonio: How does he look?

C: Not very good.

A: Describe him, please.

C: He's lying on the beach.

A: So, what's going on?

C: He has a suit of armor. He is missing a leg.

A: Ask that light (spirit) who that person is.

C: It's me! he uttered in surprise.

A: Ask that light if we can visit that life.

C: It says yes.

A: Now, I want you to float. We're going to go to that life right now, while I count from five to one. Let's leave the hunter behind. Disconnect feelings, emotions, and thoughts from that life. We are only visiting that life to get information. None of that is going to affect you. Five, four, three, two, one. You're already there. Look at your feet. What are you wearing?

C: I'm bleeding [he said, looking disgusted]. My left leg is missing.

This was exactly the leg he was having trouble with in the current life.

A: What happened to you?

C: An animal in the water.

A: What did that animal look like?

C: Big.

Note that, at no time, does he use names of species that are now familiar to us. Perhaps, at that time, the animal was not yet known and simply did not have a name. Most likely he was referring to a shark. This shows how deep he was in the hypnotic trance and how immersed he was in that life.

A: And where were you? On a boat or something?

C: Yes. I didn't want to be there.

A: Why didn't you want to be there?

C: Because I wasn't happy.

A: Why weren't you happy?

C: I was treated very badly.

A: Who treated you like that?

C: The captain.

A: So, because you were treated badly?

C: I jumped! [he said, interrupting me]. I don't regret it. Even though I'm hurt now, I'm happier.

A: Who else is on that beach where you are?

C: No one.

A: Do you know how to treat that wound?

C: No.

A: What do you plan to do now?

C: Die.

A: Is this where you're going to die?

C: I'm happy.

A: What makes you happy about dying?

C: I won't have to be with them anymore.

A: What didn't you like about them?

C: The beatings. They wouldn't give me food.

A: This was kind of a big ship?

C: Yes.

A: And what was the function of that ship?

C: To conquer.

A: Interesting. And, when you were conquering, how did you treat people before you jumped off that boat?

C: I didn't like what they were doing [referring to his companions].

A: What were they doing?

C: They were killing.

A: Do you remember the captain's name?

C: James.

A: While you are on that beach, move to the moment when you get out of that body. As you come out of the body, tell me what your thoughts are.

C: I feel happy now. I don't have to suffer for it anymore. I'd rather be dead than work and kill people.

A: What lesson do you think you had to learn in that life?

C: Sacrifice.

A: Did you pass that lesson?

C: Yes.

A: You also lived a life as a hunter prior to this one. As the hunter you were upset that people in shining armor took your wife and daughter. Now, you have been reincarnated as one of them, a man in shining armor.

C: Yes.

A: So, you have been able to experience how it feels when you are treated badly and how it feels when you treat people badly. As you can see, this is like a movie, a play. In one life you learned how it feels to be treated badly and in the other, you were in a position where you had to treat people badly, even though you didn't like it. So, what advice would you give Chris, based on the life you just lived?

C: To escape something, something else has to happen, even though that something else seems negative. It's better than where you were.

A: So, in your life, to escape something you didn't like, what did you have to sacrifice?

C: My leg [taking a deep breath and getting emotional and referring to the accident that had made it impossible for him to play baseball professionally].

A: So now Chris is thinking that, in order to escape from what he doesn't like, he has to sacrifice his leg again. Does that make sense?

C: What's happening now is not as bad as it was before.

A: Right, but do you think that in order to escape the situation you're in, and that you don't like, that you have to sacrifice your leg?

C: No.

A: Can you explain that to Chris? He doesn't need to sacrifice his leg this time. He's not the man in shining armor.

So, after a few more minutes, I began to bring Chris out of the trance he was in. His session had been fantastic, and he had been able to get the answers he was looking for.

The interesting thing about his experience is that during his life as a hunter he had more than likely felt hatred and judged the men in shining armor who had taken his wife and daughter. Then, it was his turn to be reincarnated as one of them, so he could experience both sides of the coin. Karma is not a punishment, but the law of balance. In this case, Chris was able to experience emotions from two perspectives.

From those two perspectives, he was able to find the origin of the immense sadness he felt and also the reason why he had suffered an accident in the same leg that was missing in the life of the man who had jumped off the boat. Perhaps, on a subconscious level, he had caused the accident to himself to escape his situation: having to play baseball professionally to make others happy.

Accidents are not really accidents. They serve a function, and we ourselves have the power to use them to change the course of the lessons we have come to learn. We could say that an accident could also be used as an option to activate plan B of the lesson we had originally planned.

SOUL ENTRAPMENT

During these last few years of practicing hypnosis, I have witnessed people who return to a traumatic event experience almost instant relief from the symptom they had. It could be anything from a pain in the neck or a skin rash, to problems speaking in public, or a strong terror of the dark. Many of these medically and psychologically inexplicable symptoms people brought to their hypnosis sessions were associated with a past event, speaking in linear time and existences in other bodies.

It didn't take long for me to realize that the symptom is actually the thread that takes us back to the original experience that caused it, whether in this life, during childhood, the intrauterine or womb stage, as well as in a past life or even after detaching from that physical body. But it was not until I got to know the work of the Argentinean hypnotherapist José Luis Cabouli and trained with him in his technique Past Life Therapy (TVP in Spanish) that I was able to better understand this concept called soul entrapment.

And what does soul entrapment consist of? How can the soul become 'entrapped'? Using the ideas explained above, that the soul does not understand time because for it everything is happening now; multisimultaneity; how traumas are recorded in the subconscious mind and that this survives the body and continues with the soul; and the fragmentation of the soul will all allow us to understand the concept more easily.

Soul entrapment is generated when the soul has not been able to completely process a traumatic event. The unfinished event is what generates the symptoms we may be experiencing now. When the soul does not process the traumatic event on a physical, emotional, and spiritual level, then part of it will remain trapped in that experience causing the soul to experience it as if it is still happening, even though it occurred in another body and another lifetime.

Generally, what I have found is that such entrapment takes place during the death and agony of the body in a past life when the soul cannot process that death correctly from the three levels mentioned in the previous paragraph. However, entrapment can occur at other times, not only at death. If we go back to the example of John's past life, which I described in the chapter *The Illusion of Time* and which we discussed when explaining the concept of multisimultaneity, we could say that as John had a traumatic death in Egypt part of his soul became trapped in that experience, originating the claustrophobia that he still experiences.

But why would we say that John did not process his death correctly? I will explain the concept of entrapment with an example below, but let's start by understanding that with death we solve nothing. As my teacher José Luis Cabouli says, "no one becomes a saint by dying." What this means is that dying does not automatically make us pass all the lessons we planned before we reincarnated. It will not resolve all the conflicts we have with others, we will not have a better understanding of forgiveness, nor will it remove the traumas generated in that lifetime. Death is only a change of state. What the human being sees as the death of the body, the spirit sees as a rebirth in the spirit world, to which we return with all our emotional baggage and unfinished business.

What usually happens during a traumatic death is that a kind of tunnel vision is generated, that is, we only focus on certain things that are happening, taking away the opportunity to see all the events as a whole and at the same time. Going back to John's example, let's say that in his life in Egypt, he had a wife and two children whom he loved very much. As soon as he realized that he was going to be locked in the tomb with his master and other servants, he started to panic thinking about his wife and children. He would surely think the following:

"What is going to happen to my wife?"

"Who is going to take care of my children?"

"I can't leave my children stranded."

"I need to stay to protect them."

"I will always be with them."

While he is thinking all this, his body is dying. He is not becoming aware of all that is going on with him. Even as his body dies, his last thought about his wife may be, "I promise I will always be with you." Once the body is dead, his soul departs from it without having been able to do everything it needed to do to close the cycle completely in that life.

What else would John's soul have needed to do during his death in Egypt besides becoming aware of the death of the body? We could begin by becoming aware of what his body was feeling as it was dying: the lack of air, the feeling of the lungs ceasing to function, the heart stopping, and the brain in turn not receiving the oxygen it needs to continue functioning. We could go on saying that perhaps he needed to say goodbye to his wife and children, to explain to them why he was being buried with his master, to forgive those who were locking him there, among other things.

All this is perhaps what John would have needed to do in his life in Egypt to complete the experience, thus avoiding the entrapment of his soul.

Types of Entrapment:

Past Life Entrapment

While we are using the term past lives so as not to confuse the reader, it is understood that for the soul these are not in the past and are happening now on a different timeline, so to speak. The entrapment in past lives is usually associated with the agony of the body, with what could not be completed at that time.

In the therapeutic work I do during a hypnosis session, I give the soul the opportunity to become aware of what happened in that experience and help it to complete what it could not, what was pending, both while it was in the body and when it was detached from it. One of the objectives after allowing it to complete the experience is to help it become aware that the body has died and that none of it belongs to it anymore. With this I seek to cut the connection to that life in order to end the symptom. If we look at it from John's example, this would be equivalent to cutting the connection, the network cable that links this computer to the server, in other words, disconnecting the symptoms of that life from John's soul.

To complete the experience that had been left pending, it is necessary for the person to relive everything that happened, but this time in the company of the therapist. To desensitize the trauma, it must be experienced to some degree once again. During this process of reliving that past life, I not only ask about the mental, emotional, and physical reactions, but I help the person to understand how what happened is affecting their current life, what it makes them do and what it prevents them from doing. During the death I help them become aware of what each part of their body felt, what they were thinking in those last seconds, as it could lead to *post mortem* entrapment.

The Innocent Mother

Rachel came in for consultation to work on certain symptoms that were keeping her from living fully. Among them were her anxiety when talking to people, feeling a constant lump in her throat, eye allergies, and a frequent lack of energy. Once in a trance, she began by visiting a memory from her childhood when she was six years old and in school.

In it, the teacher asked her to do a math exercise on the blackboard, but she didn't know what to do. "I don't know how to do anything," she told me.

Rachel: She would like me to do something, but since I don't know how to do anything, she gives me ugly looks and scolds me.

Antonio: And what do you feel when she scolds you?

R: A lot of shame because I'm in front of everyone. I feel ashamed.

A: In what part of your body do you feel that shame?

R: In my heart. In my chest [she answered in a soft voice].

A: And, if you knew what that felt like in your chest, in your heart, the same or similar to what would it be?

R: Like fire.

This feeling of fire would be what would take us to the original experience.

A: That's right! Very good! Feel that fire in your chest. And, if you knew where you were while you were feeling that fire in your chest, even if you think it's nonsense, where would it be?

R: I don't know where I am.

A: What do you see around you?

R: I don't know where I am. I just see like I'm inside the fire.

A: And what do you feel while you are inside the fire?

R: I see everything orange.

A: What else is going on?

R: I see people.

Rachel had reached the origin of the symptom. Apparently, she had gone back to the moment of her death in a past life where she was being burned. This was just a guess, but now we had to find out what had been the trigger for this type of death.

A: Now, I'm going to count from three to one and you're going to go back to the beginning of this experience, before you were in that fire. Three, two, one. You're already there. What's happening?

R: I see myself in a cave. It is dark.

A: Do you have the body of a male or a female?

R: A young woman.

A: What are you wearing?

R: Like a brown robe.

A: And what are you doing in that cave?

R: Waiting, [she said in a sad voice]. My hair is long and yellow.

A: And, if you knew, what would you say you were waiting for?

R: I feel locked in there.

A: You feel that confinement. What do you feel being locked in there?

R: Uncertainty.

A: Why are you locked in there?

R: I'm locked in there and I don't know why. Waiting for someone to come.

A: Move forward a little more. Go on.

R: There are more people in the cave next door. I feel pain in my neck and I'm afraid.

A: What is causing that pain in your neck?

R: It's like a bad premonition.

Rachel had gone back to the time when she and other people were locked in some kind of cave waiting for something. Now, we had to find out why they were locked in there. What had they committed to be locked in there?

A: Now, I want you to go to the previous instant that they put you in that cave. You'll go even further back. I'll count from three to one. Three, two, one. You're already there. What's happening?

R: I'm in my house with children and they're coming for me.

A: Are those children yours?

R: I think so. There is one and a baby too. They are coming for me. My house is far away and they take me. My children are crying [she recounted sadly].

A: Who is coming for you?

R: People. Men.

A: And why do they come for you?

R: They scold me. They tell me I am doing bad things.

Doesn't this scene resemble the event you experienced with her teacher at school when she was a child?

A: What bad things do they say you are doing?

R: That I talk to the moon.

A: And, when you talk to the moon, what do you talk about?

R: I like to talk to the moon. It tells me what to do. When to plant, when to have the babies.

A: And, about those babies, could you look at the big one? Look into his eyes. Have you seen those eyes before?

R: Luis [she answered, referring to his son in her present life].

A: Look at the other baby. Look at his eyes. Have you seen them before?

R: No.

A: So, men come after you and take you away. What things do they say to you?

R: They call me crazy. They tell me I don't know anything. They push me and take me to that house.

A: How do you feel when they push you and treat you like that?

R: Humiliated. I feel sorry for my children because they were left alone. My stomach hurts.

A: What is the reason for that pain in your stomach?

R: The anguish of leaving them alone, not knowing what will happen to them.

A: That's right! You feel more of that anguish in your stomach. What else is going on?

R: They're just taking me there to lock me up.

A: You're in the cave now. Go forward a little further until they pull you out. Three, two, one. You're already there.

R: They take me to that place where there are a lot of people.

A: What do these people say or do?

R: They push me and call me crazy.

A: And how do you feel when they call you that?

R: I feel humiliated. I feel afraid.

This was exactly what she had felt when the teacher sent her to the blackboard and gave her an ugly look.

A: That's it! You feel that humiliation and fear. Where do you feel it?

R: In my back and in my chest. I can't move my hands. They are tied up.

A: Go on.

R: They look at me in disgust. I am scared. I feel like I haven't done anything wrong and I don't even know what they are talking about [she said through tears]. It's like they are accusing me of things I haven't done.

A: And so far, what would you say is the most difficult moment of this experience?

R: The separation from my children.

A: I'm going to count from three to one, and you're going to go back to the moment when you separate from them. Allow your body to feel and do whatever it needs to do to relive this more deeply. Three, two, one. You are already there. What is happening?

R: I can't leave them, they're going to die! [she exclaimed, bursting into tears]

A: And while this is going on, what are your physical reactions?

R: I feel a lot of pain in my chest and stomach.

A: And while you feel that pain in your chest and stomach, what are your emotional reactions?

R: They stay crying [she said without answering the question].

A: And what are your mental reactions, as you feel them start crying and you feel that pain in your chest and stomach?

R: I don't know what is going to happen to them.

A: And all these feelings that you're telling me about, how do they affect your life as Rachel? What do they make you do?

R: Continue to support them [she replied, referring to her son in her current life].

A: What does this stop you from doing?

R: My life [she said crying]. I feel like I can't leave them.

A: Now, I want you to fast forward again to the time when you find yourself on that stage with your hands tied and people are saying things to you. Three, two, one. You're already there. What's going on?

R: They are yelling at me and throwing things at me, [she says, crying deeply.] I feel that they don't understand my pain, that they are very cruel.

A: While that is happening, what are your physical reactions?

R: I feel pain in my stomach and a lot of fear.

A: What are your emotional reactions?

R: I shake a lot [she said with difficulty breathing].

A: And what are your mental reactions?

R: I don't want to die! Who is going to take care of my children?

A: Move forward to when this experience ends. Three, two, one. Tell me what is happening now.

R: I look at my burned body.

A: Before that. Go to the instant they set the fire.

It is important to bring them to the death experience so they become aware that the body died and thus end the symptoms.

A: What is happening?

R: Someone is shouting, 'Let her burn in hell! Let her die! We don't want to see her! Let them light the fire!'

A: Let me know the moment they are lighting the fire.

R: They are lighting it.

A: I'm going to count from three to one; when I get to one, you will feel the fire touching your body more intensely. Three, two, one. Let your body feel everything it has to feel. What is happening?

R: I feel an infernal heat. It hurts.

At this point I began to ask the necessary questions to make Rachel aware of what each part of her body experienced, asking questions about what she felt, starting with her feet, so as to end the entrapment. It got to a point where she told me that she no longer felt anything.

When I asked her about what she felt in her throat, she told me that she had a rope tied around her neck, making her throat feel closed. This would explain the lump-in-the-throat sensation she referred to during the interview. When I asked her about her eyes, she told me that they were burst.

Now I had to help her soul complete all that had been left unfinished that had caused her soul to be trapped in that experience.

A: Now, I want you to talk to those people who have burned you. Tell them what you want to tell them.

R: They are ignorant. 'You know nothing. You don't know anything. You don't know about people's pain.'

A: I want you to ask them for the energy they stole from you when they burned your body.

R: Give me back the energy they stole from me. It is my energy and I want it now. It belongs to me and I want it now.

A: Now, reach out your hand and receive that energy, also the energy of that body that died. Receive it and take it into your heart. Integrate it again, feeling complete.

There was only one more step to go, to say goodbye to her children. This was related to the anguish she felt.

A: Now talk to those children you were forced to leave.

R: Forgive me [she said, bursting into tears] It wasn't my fault, my children. I did not want to leave you, my beautiful children. I did not want to leave you.

A: Tell them that you have to stay away from them for a while, but that from the light you will take care of them.

R: I have to go, but I'll be watching over them, I love them! [she said, crying more deeply now]

Coming out of the trance and evaluating that past life, Rachel brought her spirit into the light, ending that experience for good. We had found the origin of the symptoms she had brought to the session. The anxiety (related to leaving her children), the fear of speaking in public (due to being burned and humiliated in public), the eye allergy (possibly due to the eyes bursting from the fire) and the lump in her throat (related to the rope around her neck).

Spirit does not understand time. Although Rachel was only a child when she had the experience with her teacher in front of her classmates, her spirit remembered what she had experienced in that life in which she was burned alive. Being trapped in that experience, to her soul, that was still happening.

So, could we say that Rachel was born with those symptoms? I would venture to say no. What happened, as with any trauma, is that the event with the teacher triggered the memory of that life. As she stood in front of her classmates, while her teacher asked her to do something and gave her the ugly look, her soul activated the same symptoms of that past life.

The Girl on the Bus

During one of the Introspective Hypnosis trainings I taught online, I noticed that Victoria, a Russian national, showed a facility for going into a deep trance as we performed some hypnosis exercises. On the last day, which was dedicated to participants facilitating hypnosis sessions as therapists and as clients, I witnessed Victoria go to a past life in which she had had a traumatic death. The agony of the body was difficult and for that reason I decided to take control of the session to help her.

Although I had accomplished a lot in that session, I felt that Victoria still had some work to do. So I offered her a free Introspective Hypnosis session to help her finish the unfinished business her soul had.

During the interview, Victoria mentioned that she usually had anger, was easily irritated, suffered from digestive problems, and could not stand noises. She lived in the country. Her house was somewhat distant from her neighbors, but just hearing the tractor engine in the distance made her despair. She told me that on one occasion she had tried to live in the city, but it was impossible. She could not tolerate the noise of the street. There were times when she ended up on her knees on the ground crying, while she covered her ears because she could not stand the noise of the environment.

Below, I share the dialogue of her trance session:

Antonio: I will count from five to one, and as I do so you will look for a sad memory. When I get to one you'll be there. Five, four, three, two, one. You're already there. [I quickly began to see her face change expression. I asked her to make contact with that emotion.]

Victoria: I feel nauseous.

A: And while you're feeling nauseous, where are you?

V: I'm on the bus with my mom [she answered with a gesture of discomfort].

A: Okay. How old are you there?

V: Five.

A: What's your name there? [I asked, trying to figure out if it was a memory of this life or a past one]

V: Victoria [she answered, breathing a little faster].

A: Why are you feeling dizzy?

V: Oh, because of the smell of smoke and fuel. The road is up in the mountains [she said, referring to the altitude sickness]. Oh, God! It's horrible. I feel sick to my stomach. They're stopping the bus for me. I'm going to get off and throw up.

A: Alright. Now I want you to go to the first moment when you felt the same way. Let your body feel everything. Three, two, one. How does this start, what's happening, what's the first thing you feel?

V: Oh, I feel my stomach...

A: While you feel that in your stomach, what do you hear around you?

V: People screaming, attacking on their horses [she described with a horrified expression].

A: Why are people screaming?

V: Because they are attacking on horseback. There are people on horses.

Victoria was already in a past life. She had gone to the root of the same discomfort she felt on the bus as a child.

A: What else is going on?

V: It's a battlefield.

A: Look at your feet. What are you wearing?

V: High boots.

A: Is the body male or female?

V: Male.

A: Young or old?

V: Young. We are attacking.

A: And while you are attacking, what are you feeling?

V: The speed.

A: Focus on your stomach. How does it feel?

V: With discomfort. I'm startled. That's what's making me feel like this.

A: Go ahead a little bit. What else is going on? While they're riding and attacking, what's going on around you?

V: People are fighting and I'm fighting too, with sabers, [she says through tears and with a horrified expression]. The horses...

A: Feel that more and more. One. Make it more intense now. Two. Even more intense. Three. Listen to what they're saying. What are you hearing?

At this point, Victoria burst into uncontrolled crying.

V: It's crazy. People are killing each other and the horses too. Oh my God!

A: Now I want you to smell.

V: I smell blood!

A: So far, what has been the most difficult moment of this experience?

V: Having to fight and kill. What's the point of this?

A: Alright. Now I'm going to count from three to one, and you're going to head to the moment where you're killing and you're trying to make sense of it all. Let your body feel everything. Three, two, one. You are already there. While that's happening, what are your physical reactions?

V: I'm going through a group of people on horseback.

A: What is your body feeling?

V: I feel powerful and invincible.

A: And when you feel powerful and invincible, what are your mental reactions?

V: I don't care.

A: And how does all this affect your life as Victoria? You feeling powerful, invincible and not caring, what does this do to your life as Victoria?

V: That I don't care about anything. Neither my life, nor the lives of others.

A: And what does this make you do?

V: Do meaningless things. Hurting myself and others.

A: Very good. Keep attacking. What else are you feeling?

V: Oh, I think someone has hit me.

A: Where?

V: In the head.

A: I'm going to count from three to one, and when I get to one, you'll feel that hit on your head. Three, two, one. You're already there. What are you feeling in your head?

V: Pain [she answers with a groan].

A: What is the brain feeling?

V: Everything is dark.

A: What are you thinking while your head hurts and everything is dark?

V: I need air [she says, stretching her neck as if trying to take a deeper breath].

A: And, while you're feeling that, what is your throat feeling?

V: I feel like I want to throw up.

A: And what are your lungs feeling, how do they feel?

V: They are blocked.

A: Move to the moment when you leave the body, understanding that, with the death of that body that experience is over forever and none of this will ever affect you again. Three, two, one. Out of the body. Look at that body below.

Summarizing that life, what do you think you were supposed to learn?

V: It had no meaning. It had no meaning.

A: Did you learn that lesson?

V: No.

A: If you haven't learned that lesson and knowing that you're coming back as Victoria, what advice do you have for her? You know what is going on in her life.

V: Never hurt or harm just because you can.

That was how Victoria had been able to find the origin of the symptoms she had been experiencing. That which she felt as a child while on the bus awakened the memory her soul had of the life of the soldier who died in battle, feeling the speed as she rode, as she heard the screams around her and smelled the blood of the wounded.

Her soul was trapped in that life, where she had not been able to fully process the experience of her death by a blow to the head. Dying, thinking and feeling that none of it made sense, caused Victoria to feel sick to her stomach, intolerance to noises, and anger because to her soul all of this was still happening.

Helping her soul become aware of her physical, emotional, and mental reactions to that event, as well as allowing her to relive it again, made it easier for her to end that entrapment.

A few days later I was able to contact Victoria again, and this time she told me that her symptoms had completely disappeared.

Post Mortem Entrapment

As the name implies, this is the type of entrapment that occurs once the soul has been detached from the body. Remember that it is only the body that dies because for the soul life goes on. It can continue to process everything that is happening and make decisions based on that, exercising its free will.

If we look at death from the point of view of spirituality, it is at that moment that we put our entire reincarnation at risk. Not leaving the life that has just ended correctly or not accepting what it has just aroused can lead us to a state of confusion. Depending on the type of death and the emotional state in which it occurred, the soul can experience a moment of darkness and confusion that ends up making it lose the path to the light or at least make it more difficult to find it because of the darkness in which it is immersed. In my book *Guiding Lost Souls*, I talk a lot about this type of entrapment because it is very common that it makes the soul feel lost and therefore not return to the source.

When the soul leaves the body but does not go to the light, it keeps its ego, personality, beliefs, fears, and phobias. In other words it is the same person but without the body. The decisions that can be taken generally come from its ego, beliefs, and little understanding of what is happening or what has just happened. It is because of all of this that the soul can make decisions that, without realizing it, will affect it in the following incarnations.

So, what is it that can cause the soul to become trapped after death? The reasons are varied, but first it is important that we know the types of post mortem entrapment:

- **Unconscious Entrapment:** This is the type of entrapment in which the body is not conscious at the time of death. It usually occurs when life ends from one moment to the next without the soul even being aware of it. The types of deaths in these conditions can be:
    - Drug overdose
    - Coma
    - Being under the effects of anesthesia
    - Inhalation of smoke or gas
    - Heart attack
    - Tragic accident
    - Homicide

- **Conscious Entrapment:** In this entrapment, after the death of the body, the soul makes the decision to stay on this plane and not go to the light. The most common cases are:
    - Parents who stay to take care of their children.
    - Part of a couple who decides to stay to take care of their loved one.
    - Those who stay to take revenge on their enemy.
    - Those who remain attached to their material goods.
    - Those who feel they died before their time.
    - Those who feel they could not complete their projects.

- **Suicides:** Within post mortem entrapment, we could also include suicides. This case is a little different from the previous ones, since I do not consider it a conscious or unconscious entrapment. I have decided to include it within this group because the actions of the suicidal person, even before their death, trigger the same thing.

In the case of suicidal people, it is the emotional state they are in that does not allow them to see the reality of what is happening. It is as if they were in another plane, while they are immersed in sadness and depression. Moreover, what many suicidal spirits have reported is their despair at the realization that the death of the body did not solve anything, that, in fact, everything they felt before they committed suicide continued after they died. This happens because, the soul is experiencing this moment of darkness, not the body. In the case of suicide, it is the soul that decides to stop living.

Being immersed in their own darkness, suicidal people may not be able to see the light after the death of the body. That is why I say that this is not an unconscious or conscious entrapment. From my point of view, we could say that the suicidal person was already trapped in that darkness, in their own reality, even before they took their own life.

When a suicidal spirit reincarnates, it takes up again all the lessons that had been left pending. In the cases I have heard in session, I have noticed that the life of a soul who committed suicide in a past life can be complicated from an early age, as if they have additional work to do as a consequence of having taken their own life.

Below, I share excerpts from Allan Kardec's *The Spirits' Book* where spirits comment on suicide:

943. Where does the dissatisfaction with life come from, which takes hold of some individuals without any plausible reason?

"It is the effect of idleness, lack of faith, and usually, satiety. For those who employ their faculties with a useful purpose and according to their natural aptitudes, labor has nothing barren about it and life flows by more quickly. They bear life's tribulations with patience and resignation because they look forward to the more solid and lasting happiness awaiting them."

944. Do people have the right to take their own life?

"No! Only God has that right. Those who intentionally commit suicide commit a transgression against this law." – Is suicide always intentional? "Insane individuals who kill themselves do not know what they are doing."

945. What is to be thought of those who commit suicide because they are dissatisfied with life?

"Folly! Why didn't they work? Life would not have seemed so heavy to them."

The Young Girl in the Water

During the last day of class for the Introspective Hypnosis course in January 2021, Tina, who had volunteered for the demonstration session, told me that the book *Many Lives, Many Masters* by Brian Weiss was one that had meant the most to her. "I am Catherine," she told me, referring to the patient Dr. Weiss treated and whose case had been printed in his work.

Tina was referring to the number of unexplained symptoms that, like Catherine in the book, she had had. During our interview, she told me about the conditions she had experienced throughout her life. She was diagnosed with epilepsy as a child. She also suffered from episodes of suffocation and found it almost impossible to swallow. Because of that, she could not take her medications and avoided going to restaurants because she could not pass food. All of this caused panic attacks, which prevented her from leading a normal life. In addition, she was living with a breathing problem that made her feel anxious.

As soon as she entered the hypnotic trance state, I could already see tears running down her cheeks. Tina visited a sad memory where she had been afraid and felt she had to escape. She told me about the shortness of breath she began to feel as she cried inconsolably.

I decided to use this emotion to find the origin of the shortness of breath, of not being able to breathe when facing this type of situation.

Antonio: You feel you have to run away; you can't breathe, you don't know what to do. I'm going to count from three to one, and I want your soul to go to a scene where it felt the same, to the moment when all this started. Three, two, one. You're already there. If you knew, even if you think you're imagining it, how does this begin for your soul? Where are you?

Tina: I'm a little girl. I have convulsions and suddenly I stop breathing. I feel like I'm going to die [she recounted while crying deeply].

A: What is your name there? Tina?

T: Yes.

A: And how does it feel when you have these convulsions? What is your body feeling?

T: It's like I'm completely freezing.

A: And when you freeze, what do your lungs feel?

T: They're closed, totally closed, I can't breathe. I can't breathe! [bursting into tears].

A: Feel that. Feel your body freezing and your lungs not being able to breathe. I'm going to count from three to one, and I want you to go back, and further back to the time when this not being able to breathe started. Even before this life, if possible. Three, two, one. You are already there.

T: I'm in the water! [She gasped, cried, and struggled to breathe.] I'm all alone. I just fell out of the boat.

A: That's it! Feel that. In that place, do you have a man's or a woman's body?

T: A woman's. I can't swim!

A: Go on. What else is wrong?

T: Nothing. I'm going to die. I'm going to die!

A: Let that body die.

T: I try to stay on the surface, but it's impossible.

Tina's body began to contract as she experienced the death of that body in a past life, in which she was drowning.

T: I can't take it anymore! I'm so tired!

A: Just let go. Now, I'm going to count from three to one, and I want you to go to the moment when this really started. The instant before you fell off that boat. Three, two, one. You're already there. What's going on?

T: I'm in the boat. I have a beautiful, long, white dress. I'm blonde.

A: Who is with you? Is there someone with you?

T: Yes, there is a man with me. I feel like he is my husband.

A: Okay, go on. What else is going on?

T: We are on the deck arguing. I can feel that I am not happy. I am anxious and afraid.

A: What else is going on? Go on a little more.

T: I don't know, but I'm telling myself that I want to end this. I have a chance to end this for good [breaking down in tears again].

A: Go on. What else is going on?

T: It sounds crazy, but I'm jumping, I'm jumping!

A: And so far, what has been the most difficult moment of this experience?

T: I thought I was going to jump to save myself [she says with tears in her eyes, referring to the man she was in the boat with].

A: And, while you thought he was going to jump in to save you, what are your physical reactions at that moment?

T: I feel cold. It's cold.

A: And as you feel that cold, what are your emotional reactions?

T: I feel so lonely.

A: And while you are feeling lonely, what are your mental reactions?

T: That I wasn't worth it. It's better if I die.

A: Now, I want you to see how all this is affecting your life as Tina. When you are cold, lonely, and think you are not worth it, what does it make you do in your life as Tina?

T: It always makes me feel like I'm not worth it.

A: What does that stop you from doing?

T: I don't show myself as I am. I have so much inside of me, and I don't show it to people. I'm always hiding.

A: Now, I'm going to count from three to one. When I get to one, I want you to allow your body to feel everything it needs to feel to complete this experience forever. Now, you are going to feel yourself drowning. Three, two, one. You start drowning now.

That's how I began to ask the questions necessary for Tina, in the life of that drowning young woman, to become aware of the death of that body. I asked her what every part of her body was feeling, and every organ, while dying.

A: What are your legs feeling?

T: My legs are still struggling.

A: What are your lungs feeling?

T: My lungs are full of water already.

A: And while your lungs are full of water, feel your throat. What is your throat feeling?

T: It's closed [she is crying and having difficulty breathing]. "I can't breathe! I can't breathe!"

A: What does the brain feel while it is not getting oxygen?

T: My brain is shutting down.

A: What is the last thought you have in that brain?

T: What a waste. My life was a waste. I have wasted my life.

A: Once you are ready, let that body die and leave that body. Understand that, with the death of that body, that experience is over forever and nothing is going to affect you anymore. Now, I want you to talk to that man. What do you want to say to him?

T: It was not your responsibility to make me happy. You didn't love me, but that's okay. It's not so tragic.

A: If you were to summarize the life that just ended, what do you think you needed to learn?

T: I needed to learn that I can't expect someone to save me, that I need to feel the value of life for myself. No one can do it for me and I don't need someone to tell me.

Then, I told her that she needed to expel the water from her lungs. I asked her to turn on her side and vomit up all that water she had swallowed while drowning. That vomit was actually an energetic vomit because of the death imprint she had. The woman was also able to forgive herself for ending her life that way.

When we finished the session and she came out of the hypnotic trance, the first thing she said was that she felt her lungs open. "I can't explain it. It's so different," she told me. Tina was smiling and feeling great.

We had been able to find the origin of the feeling of suffocating and freezing, of not being able to swallow, of the panic attacks and anxiety. Her soul had been trapped in that event, which was still happening for her, thus causing all of those symptoms.

The day after the session, Tina sent me an emotional email telling me what she had felt that day after the session. She had gone to the kitchen to get something to eat and noticed that she was able to swallow without any problems. She also noticed that her muscles had relaxed and she could breathe normally. She could feel oxygen entering her lungs without any problems.

A few months later, in May 2021, when I contacted her to ask for her permission to use her real name in this case, she not only very kindly agreed but gave me an update on what she experienced after the session. This is what she wrote to me:

> *I will take this opportunity to update you on my progress. I already felt instant relief after the session. I felt as if my throat opened up, as if the muscles were constantly contracted before. I feel like my throat is wider now. Swallowing larger pieces of food is no longer a nightmare. I used to only feel 100% comfortable with creamy soups and bananas. Sounds pretty awful, I know.*
>
> *Breathing is also much better. But here comes an even better side effect. Since breathing is life, the fact that I breathe more relaxed means also living more relaxed and open. The level of joy increased a lot. Life has less limitations if you are not constantly suffocating. Less fear. And by suffocating, I mean on all levels. So now I feel like I am exploring a new way of being and relating to the world. More honest, more fluid, more open. It's a longer process, I know, but very exciting.*

Entrapment in the Womb

The time we spend in the womb and everything we experience there will have a tremendous influence on our life after birth. There are many techniques that do not take into consideration this period of our lives, but from my point of view the therapeutic work would not be complete if we do not pay attention to it, since it is necessary to know everything that our mother was experiencing at that moment in order to understand how what she felt affected us, and more importantly, how it may still affect us.

First, let us begin by understanding that our mother has her own vibrational field and we have ours, even while in her womb. The challenge for the soul inhabiting the fetus is that during this time it will feel whatever the mother experiences on a physical, emotional, and mental level, as if it were its own. It will not be able to differentiate which sensation is its own and which belongs to its mother. At birth it will forget all of that, but it will already be recorded in the subconscious mind as if it were its own experience. It could be said, in a way, that our mind is programmed by everything we experience in the womb.

To begin with, let us review all that it can bring as an incarnated spirit:

- Lessons to be learned
- Traumas
- Entrapments
- Karma with others
- The society it decided to reincarnate in
- Fears

Among other things, while pregnant, the mother may experience:

- The death of a loved one
- Abandonment by her partner
- Problems in her family environment
- Abandonment by her parents

And that is not all. The soul inside the baby in the womb has a kind of telepathic communication with its mother and can know everything she is thinking and feeling. Not only does it know what is going on with her, but also with her immediate environment. How is this possible? Several of those who went back to time in the womb have reported that they did not stay inside the baby's body all the time, but that their soul went out and came back in as it finished integrating with the baby's body.

So, what could the mother be thinking during pregnancy? Let's look at some examples I have been able to find in sessions:

- "This pregnancy is a mistake."
- "It is better to abort, as I am not ready yet."
- "Because I am pregnant my parents reject me."
- "My partner left me because I got pregnant."
- "God, please grant me a girl," when the spirit knows it is going to be a boy.

There are many other thoughts a pregnant mother might have, but let's think for a moment how in these case the baby might be affected. What might the baby be feeling or thinking?

- "I'm a mistake, and I shouldn't be here."
- "Because of me my mom is having a hard time with my grandparents."
- "Because of me my dad left my mom."
- "I'm just causing her suffering."
- "I know I'm going to be a boy, and I'm going to let mom down. When I'm born, I'll do everything I can to make it up to her."
- "I'd better not even move so they don't realize I'm here because they might kill me (abort me)."

This should give us an idea about how the baby's soul might be processing the information it is receiving. Not only will it process it, but it will influence it once it is born. For example, knowing that the mother thinks it should not be there, it could have self-esteem problems or even take an attitude of invisibility to avoid problems and confrontations without expressing what it feels and what it thinks because it does not feel entitled to do so.

If the mother is suffering because her partner abandoned her or perhaps because she has no other option but to stay with an abusive partner because she will not be able to support her baby on her own, it is most likely that, after the birth and for the rest of her life, that son or daughter will opt for a pleasing attitude towards his or her mother. Many people even feel that they have a duty to get the mother out of any difficult situation at the expense of their peace of mind or happiness, without even being aware of their behavior.

If the father said, "I don't know what I would do if it is not a girl," and the soul knows that it will be born a boy, it may also adopt a similar behavior towards the father, feeling that it has to compensate him because he was born a boy, when he wanted a girl. Moreover, the soul may even feel the need to change its sexual orientation in order to be the girl that the father wanted so much.

Those who felt the threat of being aborted may seek to avoid confrontation or arguments and try to remain unnoticed in life, unable to express their ideas, desires, or feelings. In their mind, the program "if they realize I am here, they will kill me" is always present in their subconscious because this is what they experienced and they don't realize that these emotions do not belong to them.

To end the entrapment of the soul in the womb, the soul must be helped to relive the experience, to become aware of everything that happened there and how it is affecting it in its present life. The next step is to seek to disconnect those emotions, thoughts, or programming that actually belong to the mother.

Emma in Her Mother's Womb

When I asked her what it was that needed to heal her soul that day, Emma, a young South African girl, replied, "getting upset when I'm not listened to, having to fight for my truth." She also mentioned that she had always felt the need to protect her mother and to seek love and approval from her father.

Already in a hypnotic trance, we explored what she felt when she was not listened to and had to fight for her truth. Emma returned to a not-too-distant memory in which her employer was accusing her of something she had not done.

Emma: He is raising his voice and telling me that it is my fault, and I tell him that it is not.

Antonio: And at this moment when he is raising his voice at you saying that it is your fault, what are you feeling?

E: Anger and frustration.

A: That's right. You feel that anger and frustration more intensely. Where in your body do you feel that anger and frustration?

E: In my gut.

A: Okay, experience that in your gut. And what is that feeling similar to, like what is happening to your gut?

E: Guilt and lack of confidence.

A: And this feels like what?

E: Like being punched.

A: I'm going to count from three to one, and I want you to go to another time when you've felt the same way, accused and that feeling in your gut like you're being punched. Three, two, one. You're already there. If you knew, even if you think you're imagining it, where are you now?

E: At home, in the backyard with my dad.

A: What's going on?

E: He tells my brother and me that we broke something, but we didn't break it.

A: How old are you?

E: Nine.

A: Alright, go on. Repeat what he is saying to you.

E: He says, 'I know you have broken this, and your mother is not here.' He picks up a rake and hits us both in the legs with it.

A: How do you feel when your father is accusing you of breaking that?

E: Wounded.

A: Where do you feel that in your body?

E: In my heart.

A: Alright, I'm going to count from three to one, and I want you to go to the first time you experienced that in your heart and in your gut. Three, two, one. You're already there. Like you know, what's going on now?

E: I'm at my aunt and uncle's house, and we're playing. I want to stay, but my dad says I can't, so I run away. When I come back, he hits me with some plastic.

A: How old are you there?

E: Seven.

A: Okay, what is your father saying to you while he is hitting you with that plastic?

E: 'I told you not to leave.'

A: Now I'm going to count from three to one, and I want you to go to the beginning of all this between your soul and your father's soul. Go backwards, maybe to before you were born. Three, two, one. You are already there. If you knew, even if you think you're making it up, how does this start between you and your father?

E: I don't know.

A: And if you did know, imagine even before you were born.

E: He wanted a boy, and he had a girl.

A: That's it, alright. Now I want you to go to the time in your mother's womb as I count from three to one. Three, two, one. You're already there. You can feel it or you can imagine it. Right now you are in your mother's womb, and you are connected to her. You can feel what she feels, think what she thinks. What is your mother feeling while you are in her womb?

E: Love and protection.

A: What is going on with her or around her?

E: Her sister is living with her, and my dad pushes her down the stairs.

A: Who is he pushing, your mom?

E: Yes. [She answered with tears in her eyes.]

A: I'm going to count from three to one, and I want you to repeat the first words that come out of your father before he pushes your mother down the stairs. Three, two, one. What is your father saying?

E: 'I hate you!'

A: And while your father is saying that, what do you feel?

E: I feel unloved [she said, crying].

A: Now I want you to move forward to the moment when your mother rolls down the stairs, allowing your body to feel everything it needs to feel. Three, two, one. What do you feel as you roll down the stairs with your mother?

E: I'm bouncing with the hope that my mom is okay.

A: And how does that make you feel?

E: I just want her to be okay.

A: What does your mom say to your dad while she's on the floor?

E: She's upset and says, 'How dare you hurt me!'

A: How do you feel when she says that?

E: I want to protect her, but I can't.

A: Now move forward to another significant event during your time in your mother's womb. Three, two, one. You're already there. What's happening?

E: I feel safe because my mother is alone.

A: Now move forward to another significant event in your mother's womb. Three, two, one.

E: I am wondering if I am a burden and if I am unwanted.

A: What makes you say that?

E: She told me I wasn't planned, but she loves me anyway.

A: And what makes you think you are a burden?

E: Why would my father push us down the stairs? [She bursts into tears.]

A: I want you to go a little further. Three, two, one. You're already there.

E: I remember when they want to pick my name. My mother chose a terrible name. [She laughed.]

A: Does your father know you're going to be a girl?

E: No, he doesn't. He's expecting a boy.

A: And while your father is expecting a boy, and you know you're a girl, how does that make you feel?

E: It makes me want to be the boy he wants.

With this Emma had found the origin of her father's mistreatment and of always going out to protect her mom, constantly seeking her father's approval and admiration. From the time in the womb, she had made the decision to be that boy that her father so much hoped for and that was going to be the behavior she would take from birth.

A: So far, what has been the most difficult moment during your time in the womb?

E: Feeling that my father was trying to get rid of both of us.

A: And in the moment when he is trying to get rid of the two of you, what are your physical reactions?

E: I want him to be happy with me. I want him to love me. [She said in tears.]

A: And when you want him to love you, what are your emotional reactions?

E: Fear that he won't love me.

A: When you feel that fear that he won't love you, what are your mental reactions?

E: Pain.

A: Where do you feel that pain?

E: In my heart and in my head.

A: Now, I want you to see how all this is affecting your life as Emma.

E: It causes me to shut down and not let other people into my life.

A: And what does this stop you from doing?

E: Loving others, helping other people, letting them into my life.

A: Now I want you to go back to the moment before you entered your mother's womb. Three, two, one. This is the moment before you entered your mother's womb. I want you to share with me why you are choosing those parents. What is it that your soul needs to learn through them?

E: To love.

And so, Emma's session continued, helping her to experience her birth, to become aware of all that had happened, and to do all that she had not been able to do at the time. Emma, a newly born baby, was able to talk to her mother and explain that she could no longer protect her because it had been her decision to stay with her father despite the way he treated her.

When I asked her to talk to her dad explaining that she was a child and that she was perfect the way she was, she said:

E: Just love me the way I am, Dad. I love you even though I'm not your little boy. I am your little girl who loves you and wants to be like you.

Entrapment During Birth

One of the most traumatic experiences for the soul is that of birth. That moment may remind the soul of the agony of another body. The sensation of constriction as it moves through the birth canal may remind it of a life where it has experienced confinement or been buried alive. Manipulation with forceps, for example, may remind you of a life in which you were tortured. If the baby is placed in an incubator after birth, it may evoke a death in which it was locked or trapped.

On the other hand, what the mother says or does after the baby is born is also relevant. Whether or not she was able to hold it in her arms, if she was put to sleep under general anesthesia, if she was immediately separated from the baby to be placed in an incubator, among other scenarios. All of this hurts and programs us.

If the mother is asleep under anesthesia, the baby may think he killed the mother when he was born. If the mother could not hold the baby because he was immediately put in an incubator, he may feel the anxiety of separation and not being accepted. All of these examples have been real situations that I have experienced with patients I have facilitated hypnosis sessions for.

The Legless Miner

Soukaïna took the Introspective Hypnosis course in 2020. During the practices, I noticed that she easily went into trance. Her simplicity and sweet character could not hide the marks of the emotions she had pending to work on. Due to the culture of her country of origin and her religion, Soukaïna experienced limitations and prohibitions for being a woman.

She demonstrated a need for approval in everything she did and a need to feel accepted. She manifested this pattern with everyone around her, but it was most marked with her mother. I will begin with one of the past lives she visited during her session.

Antonio: Tell me whatever comes to your mind, whatever you are feeling in your body or whatever emotion you are experiencing [I told her trying to create a bridge to the original experience]. What is going on?

Soukaïna: I feel that I am not enough [she answered, bursting into tears].

A: And where do you feel that in your body?

S: I feel it in my knees.

A: I want you to live that feeling more intensely. What you are feeling in your knees feels, like what is happening to them?

S: They are trapped.

A: I'm going to count from three to one, and I want you to go to where your knees are trapped. Three, two, one. You're already there. Like you know, where are you while your knees are trapped? Where are you while you're feeling that? Tell me even if you think you're imagining it.

S: I don't know.

A: Do you feel like you are standing, sitting, or lying down?

S: I feel like there is a weight on my knees. It's like I'm being pinned down.

A: Do you feel like you are in a place or that someone is making you feel that way?

S: I am in a place. I feel like there is something very heavy on my legs, and I am not strong enough to get it off me.

A: Touch your body, is it male or female?

S: I am a young man, like 40 years old.

A: Can you move your arms?

S: No.

A: Can you hear anything around you?

S: I hear like machinery.

A: I'm going to count from three to one, and I want you to go to the time before you got to that place. Three, two, one. You're already there. What's going on?

S: I'm in a mine. I'm digging with a shovel, and I'm not alone. I'm with a team. I hear something rumbling and I look up, and rocks are falling on me. I'm trapped under the rocks and separated from the rest of the team.

A: While you're there, what are your physical reactions?

S: I can no longer feel my legs.

A: And not feeling your legs, what are your emotional reactions?

S: I'm scared [she told me, crying].

A: And when you are scared there, what are your mental reactions?

S: I'm trapped and I'm going to die in here. If I don't die, I'm going to lose my legs, and I won't be able to live that way [she replied, crying inconsolably].

A: How is all this affecting your life as Soukaïna, this not feeling your legs, being scared, and thinking you are going to die? What does all this make you do?

S: It makes me feel insecure about myself. I can't stand on my two legs. I need someone to help me.

A: What does this stop you from doing?

S: Building my own life, taking responsibility, and being free. I am not free.

A: Repeat that one more time.

S: I am not free! [She exclaimed, crying and wailing out loud.]

A: I'm going to count from three to one, and I want you to go to the moment when all these rocks start falling on you. When I get to one you will feel the impact. Allow your body to feel everything more intensely. Three, two, one. You are already there.

At that moment, Soukaïna suffered a kind of spasm while trying to take a breath with great difficulty.

A: While you are experiencing that, what do your legs feel?

S: I feel my spine breaking [she gasped with difficulty].

A: What are your lungs feeling?

S: I can hardly breathe.

A: What is your heart feeling?

S: It's beating fast.

A: What is your throat feeling?

S: I'm trying to scream, but I can't [she said, almost mumbling].

A: What is the brain feeling?

S: Panic. I'm alone [she answered, crying again].

A: Where are you?

S: In the street.

A: Why are you alone?

S: My wife left me. She got tired of taking care of me.

A: How long have you been on the street?

S: Ten years.

A: Since this is the last minute of that life, what are you feeling?

S: That I am useless.

A: And as you're dying, what's the last thought you are able to think in that brain?

S: That I am happy to be leaving this life. I am happy to die.

A: Why are you happy to die?

S: Because this world has been cruel to me.

It is important to emphasize those last sentences and thoughts, and even all the vocabulary that the miner used to describe how he felt. These are the ones that are causing the entrapment of her soul in that life by being stuck in the role of victim.

A: When you are ready get out of that body, understanding that with the death of that body, this experience is over forever, none of this is going to affect you. You don't need to carry any of this into other bodies. What do you think you had to learn in that life?

S: I had to learn to be self-sufficient.

A: Did you manage to learn that lesson?

S: No.

A: Why do you think you didn't pass it?

S: Because I gave up after my wife left.

A: So that limitation in your legs made you feel that you weren't enough and you gave up?

S: Yes. I let myself starve to death.

At this point I ask the miner's soul, which is also Soukaïna's soul, and which at that time is more connected to the spirit world, to give her advice based on her experience in the life that had just ended. This is what she said:

S: You cannot put your life in the hands of others. Your life is for you to live and build. Yes, you can have support. Yes, you can have people helping, but don't depend on that alone.

A: Is this where this life ends? In this place?

S: No.

A: I want you to move forward, but in the meantime, tell me what you are thinking.

S: I think my life is not going to be the same.

I continued to ask her questions until the miner was rescued. He had lost feeling in his legs. He told me that all this generated great insecurity and an absence of connection to the earth. The man could no longer work and felt like a burden, like an obstacle to his family.

A: How does all this make you feel?

S: Useless. I feel like I'm not enough.

A: And what does that make you do in your life as Soukaïna?

S: I stop trying.

A: And what does that stop you from doing?

S: Explore and grow.

A: I want you to move until the last moment of that life. What is happening?

This is how, after a few minutes, the miner's spirit returned to the light, closing that chapter forever and ending with the trapping of his soul. All that the miner's soul had felt, being trapped in that experience, caused Soukaïna to experience the same emotions and to be trapped in the role of victim. In the present life, she would experience situations that would allow her to complete the lessons she was unable to in the miner's life. When one does not learn a lesson in a past life, one simply repeats it. There have been several occasions when the souls of my clients have told me that they had been trying to learn a single lesson for many lifetimes.

As the soul does not understand time because for it everything happens now, we will now see how this experience in turn relates to the time when Soukaïna was in her mother's womb. Soukaïna was aware that, despite understanding what she came to learn in this life, she still felt a great need for approval.

Soukaïna in Her Mother's Womb

Antonio: Soukaïna, I want you to move forward to the moment when you are in your mother's womb before you are born. Five, four, three, two, one. You are already there. And as you re-experience that warm, moist environment, do you feel that your arms and legs are in a comfortable position?

Soukaïna: Yes

A: What about your neck, is it comfortable?

S: Yes.

A: How do your legs feel?

S: They feel like tingling.

A: Can you feel your mother's emotions?

S: Oh, yes.

A: What is she feeling?

S: Sadness.

A: What is your mother thinking?

S: That she made a mistake.

A: Since you are in the womb, you are connected to your mom. You are inside her vibratory body. Ask your mom what mistake she made.

S: 'What mistake did you make?' [she asked her starting to cry] She says she shouldn't have married my dad.

A: I see. Ask her why she is sad even though she is pregnant.

S: Because she doesn't have the courage to leave. She feels obliged to stay because of my older sister and me, more so now that I'm here.

A: And how does that make you feel?

S: Guilty, [she answered, crying more deeply].

This information provided by Soukaïna is of great value, as it gives us a clue about the cause of her soul's entrapment during the stage of her gestation.

A: And when you feel this way, what does it make you do in your life as Soukaïna?

S: Try to compensate her for it.

This would be the confirmation of the suspicion mentioned above and in fact the explanation of your behavior in life and of the need to always count on your mother's approval and to be validated by others.

A: And, when you try to make it up to your mom, what does that stop you from doing?

S: Living for myself.

A: Tell me if any of those emotions your mother is feeling are your emotions too.

S: They are all hers [she said, bursting into tears].

A: They are all hers and because you are in there, you feel them as if they were yours. I want you to move forward to the moment when you are about to be born. I'm going to count from three to one. Let your body feel everything it needs to feel as you are being born. Three, two, one. You're already there. What's happening?

S: It's sad [she continued with an inconsolable cry]. Even though I am being born, she is sad because my father is not there.

A: And while you are being born, what are your physical reactions?

S: I feel a tingling all over my body. The first breath I take is burning my lungs. It is very cold.

A: What are your emotional reactions while you are being born?

S: I am confused.

A: And what are your mental reactions while you are being born?

S: I am curious. I look around me and I see shadows, things moving that don't feel familiar.

A: I want you to pay attention to what they are saying around you. What are they saying?

S: The doctor is laughing, and he is trying to make my mother laugh to lighten her mood.

A: And what is your mom doing?

S: She is laughing, but I can sense that she is very sad.

A: Is your mom holding you?

S: Yes.

A: And as she holds you in her arms, what are you feeling?

S: That she is sorry. She knows that we are going to suffer because the relationship with my father is not a peaceful relationship.

A: You are right. It is her relationship with your father, and you have nothing to do with it. Now, I want you to locate your umbilical cord, and in a moment I'm going to count from three to one. When I get to one, you will be able to cut the cord. And when you cut the cord, your energy will be disconnected from your mother forever. Those emotions, that fear, that sadness are going to be disconnected forever because they belong to your mother and not to you. Three, two, one. Cut the cord now.

And, now that you have cut the cord, you are free and you can go back to being yourself, understanding that you don't have to please anyone or compensate your mother for anything. Talk to your mother and explain. From now on you are not going to feel that sadness she felt. You don't have to make her happy because you are not guilty of anything.

You will be with her because you are her daughter, but you are not going to feel her emotions. You can tell her that.

S: Mom, I love you, but I can't carry your emotions forever. I can't absorb all your pain anymore. It's not my duty, not my responsibility. I've wasted a lot of time doing that, and I've been depriving you of your own opportunity to grow. I need to start living on my own. Mom, I will always be with you, and I will always love you, but I can't fix your life. I'm sorry. [She ended with tears in her eyes.]

The session continued for a few more minutes before we brought Soukaïna out of the hypnotic trance she was in. We had found the origin of her soul entrapment. She had taken responsibility for her mother's sadness.

SOUL FRAGMENTATION

So far we have talked about how traumas affect the conscious and the subconscious mind and how all this also affects the soul. However, in the presence of a painful event, there are a whole series of consequences the soul experiences, such as soul fragmentation. In the previous chapter I explained the concept of soul entrapment and the situations in which it can occur. Fragmentation is another possible consequence of soul entrapment, but it does not mean that all entrapment results in fragmentation.

This term is not a new concept. It has been used and contemplated by shamans since ancient times. In practice, shamans acted hand in hand with the spirit world through altered states of consciousness. Several used various tools, such as tobacco smoke, the beat of a drum, fire, dances, ícaros (medicinal songs), vigils, among others. Their objective is to interact with the spirit world to find the spiritual aspect of illnesses for the recovery of the soul of the person they are helping.

During my first years of hypnosis practice, I had already heard the term fragmentation and soul retrieval, however I did not pay it the attention or interest it deserved. It was not until I met my teacher Jose Luis Cabouli that I witnessed the use of this technique in one of his workshops in Mexico. It was at this point that I understood the great therapeutic value of the recovery of soul fragments.

But what is soul fragmentation, what does it consist of, and how can the soul be fragmented? To explain this idea, let's remember first that the soul is energy, and not only energy, but energy with its own consciousness and intelligence. When we experience a shock that our soul cannot handle or process, a part of it,—the part that does not want to feel, that is frightened and does not understand what is happening—detaches from the rest and leaves. This can happen during a serious accident, sexual or emotional abuse, among other scenarios. While it is true that I have found more cases of soul fragmentation during childhood, it can happen at any time in our lives.

When the soul fragments, our life energy is trapped in that event. Fragmentation of the soul carries a variety of consequences. Here are some of them:

- The fragmented part of the soul remains at the age the person was at the time of the traumatic event, and therefore does not continue the spiritual evolution of the rest of the soul.
- By remaining trapped in that experience, no matter how much time has passed, that part will continue to make us feel everything it felt and is still feeling because for that fragmented area, it is happening now.
- We lose access to that part of our energy. In other words, as the soul fragments, we no longer have access to 100% of our soul. For example, if in fragmentation the soul loses 10% of its energy, that would leave us with 90% of our energy. Now if we were to think about how many times our soul may have fragmented in this life alone, we can understand how much of that energy we do not have access to and how many symptoms it may be causing us.

And if we talk about loss of energy in the fragmentation of the soul, there are other types of effects:

- Having lost access to a percentage of our energy, we may experience chronic fatigue or exhaustion.
- In addition, we would look like Swiss cheese, with holes in it. This in turn weakens the aura, which is the natural shield we rely on to protect us from external energies, including lost souls who want to attach themselves to our energy field.

- By not having all of our energy with us, we feel incomplete. Some people may experience confusion.
- Some may experience a disconnection from the body's sensations and emotions. People who did not know they had a fragmented soul have told me things like, *"I don't feel in my body all the time,"* or *"I can think love, but I can't feel it."*

Therefore it is essential to recover the fragments of the soul and re-integrate them into us, not only to recover our energy but also because in that way we would be working on our traumas. For example, shamans perform a shamanic journey in which they themselves search for the fragments of the soul in order to return them to the body of their patient. Nowadays, by combining the use of hypnosis with shamanic concepts, we can make the person themselves go in search of their soul fragments.

What Symptoms Can a Person With a Fragmented Soul Experience?

Scientifically we cannot prove it, but based on what we have found in sessions with our clients, we could mention the following:

- Lack of energy
- Chronic fatigue
- Vulnerable to external energies including lost souls
- Not feeling present at all times
- Feeling disconnected from the physical body
- Confusion

Difference Between Entrapment and Fragmentation of the Soul

After talking about soul entrapment, confusion may arise because it seems that in a way we are talking about the fragmentation of the spirit. While it is true that the two concepts may be similar, since in both the soul and our energy are affected by trauma, causing various symptoms, the difference lies in the following points:

- Soul fragmentation is the detachment of a portion of our soul, as if we were dividing our energy into smaller parts. In entrapment, the soul energy is 100% complete.
- Entrapment is generated when the soul has something pending completion in some traumatic event. Fragmentation of the soul causes a fragment to break off and leave because it cannot withstand the pain or intensity of that event.
- To reintegrate the fragments, therapeutic work must first be completed to initiate recovery, while entrapment ends when the soul can complete the experience.

Fragmentation Is One of the Consequences of Entrapment

Fragmentation can occur in the present life, in the womb, in a past life, or even after death in a past life. The difference is that if the fragmentation happened in a past life, when the soul returns to the light, the fragments are re-integrated. That is why when we work with soul fragmentation, we refer to current life events.

Going back to John's past life chart, we look at entrapment in the following way:

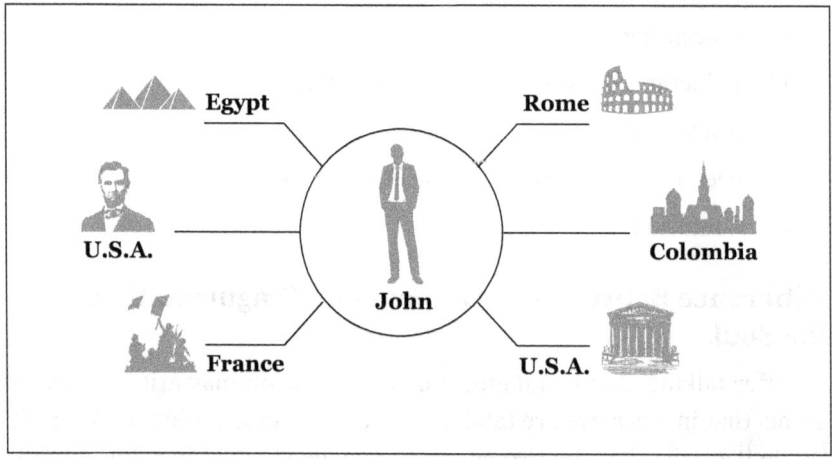

Let's look at John and at his past lives, which are happening 'now' from the point of view of soul time, quantum time. We could say that part of John's energy (soul) was trapped in the Egyptian life. His soul is not fragmented, but the entrapment causes him to be connected to that life, transmitting the symptoms.

Continuing with this example, imagine another connection to the life of Rome, where he died being attacked by a lion; another to the life of France, where he died in battle; and another to life in the United States, where he also died on a battlefield. Now, let's add another connection to a life in which a soul entrapment originated. This occurred in the womb, where he felt that his mother was thinking of aborting him and that his father wanted the baby to be a girl, when he knew it was going to be a boy. Finally, the spirit has multiple connections.

Is it understood, then, how our soul can be caught up in different events at the same time? This does not mean that we are fragmented, just connected to those events and making us feel all that we feel in the present. We have all our energy with us, but we do not have access to the part of the energy that was trapped in that event.

The Girl in the Room

Roxana is a young South American girl who lived through an atrocious experience that resulted in the fragmentation of her soul. She was abused by her grandfather when she was just a child.

Sadly, this story is just one of many I encountered in my practice. Cases of rape and molestation of minors perpetrated by people close to their family circle are very common to hear in session. I will delve more into this topic and the effects this type of abuse can have later in the chapter *Rape and Molestation*.

Roxana came to the session feeling depressed, with low self-esteem, disconnected from her feelings, and had been experiencing seizures recently. Already in a trance state, Roxana returned to an event in her current life when she was three years old. She was lying alone in her parents' bed and waking up from a nap. Like any baby, she started crying, waiting for her parents to come and attend to her, but it was her grandfather who arrived. Below, I share part of the dialogue:

Roxana: Right now, I am alone. I cry, but nobody comes.

Antonio: Very good. Go on a little more. Feel that sadness and that loneliness. Let the baby feel all that.

R: I cry, but no one comes, [she said, crying inconsolably].

A: Continue.

R: No!

A: What is going on?

R: No!

A: Go on. Allow your body to feel everything it needs to feel.

A: What's happening?

R: My grandfather comes in [she answered crying, as if knowing what was about to happen]. Then I stop crying and close my eyes.

A: Yes, continue.

R: I pretend I'm asleep so he'll go away. No!

A: That's it. Keep going. What's going on?

R: He starts putting his hands on me. I don't like it. I don't like his smell.

A: Continue. What else is going on?

R: He's touching me down there with his fingers. He's hurting me.

A: Go on some more.

R: I try not to cry too hard and I tune out. I leave.

Here Roxana was referring to the fragmentation of her soul.

A: And how do you disconnect?

R: I don't know. I go somewhere else.

A: Continue from wherever you are. Tell me what happens to your body.

R: It hurts so I go away so I don't have to feel it anymore.

A: That's it. Continue.

R: And I don't come back until it's gone.

A: Move until the moment it's gone. What's happening now?

R: He hugs me and wets me.

A: What is he wetting you with?

R: He's behind me! I don't know.

A: Continue. Let your body feel everything and continue.

R: It's so disgusting. He will never leave me alone.

Here, Roxana was confirming that this had not been the first time her grandfather had abused her.

A: Go a little further. See what happens next.

R: I think he's zipping up his pants.

A: Go on.

R: I wrap myself in the blanket and go again.

Roxana says this again referring to the fragmentation of her soul.

A: Continue.

R: He leaves, and I wake up again. When I finally get out of bed and go to the other room, no one notices me.

A: How do you feel when no one notices you?

R: Sad.

A: So far, what has been the most difficult moment of this experience?

R: Everything.

A: And, when you find yourself in that experience, what are your physical reactions as your grandfather does that to you?

R: I want to throw up. I feel disgusting. I feel dirty.

A: And what are your emotional reactions?

R: I want to run away and hide. I want to cry and scream [she answered in tears].

A: And when you want to run away, you want to hide, cry and scream, what are your mental reactions?

R: I feel hurt, how can you do this to me!

A: Now I want you to see how all this is affecting your life as Roxana. When you say you want to vomit, that you feel disgusting and dirty, wanting to run away, to hide, to run and scream.

R: I feel hurt.

A: And what does that do to you in your life as Roxana?

R: Pretending it didn't happen.

A: When you pretend that didn't happen, what does that stop you from doing?

R: Facing it.

Roxana's session continued for a few more minutes. After helping her understand what had happened to her and how it was all hurting her life, I proceeded to help her desensitize the trauma, that is to help her soul complete all that it could not do at the time, and then proceed to recover the fragments of her soul.

It was this fragmentation that had taken place on several occasions that made her feel disconnected, depressed, and caused her to experience the seizures. Part of her soul had been trapped in that event and in the age it happened, causing her the symptoms mentioned today.

Later, in the chapter *Male and Female Energies*, I will explain in more detail the after-effects that a rape causes in the soul. For now, the only thing I wish to show with this case is how the soul fragments in the face of a traumatic event.

TYPES OF DEATH AND THEIR SYMPTOMS

Throughout my years of hypnosis practice, I have witnessed that most of the unexplained symptoms my clients have experienced during their lifetimes were related to the time of death of the body in a previous life. Depending on the level of trauma at death, the soul can become trapped and bring all that it felt during the death of that body into the present body. For this reason, the golden rule in any past life regression is to navigate a past life up to the time of the death of the body, as it will help us understand not only how it died and what symptoms it may have generated, but what led the person to die that way.

The interesting thing in these cases is that everything the soul drags to the new body is stored at a subconscious level, and therefore the person cannot have access to it. This means that when the person (the soul) experiences a similar situation, either physically, mentally, or emotionally, to the one he or she experienced at that time, the symptoms will be triggered automatically without the person understanding the reason for his or her reaction, behavior, or pain. The soul will experience everything it experienced in that event, as if it were happening right now.

Many of my clients decided to have a hypnosis session as a last resort, after having sought the answer and cure for their ailments in traditional medicine. This is not to say that all of our symptoms come from past lives or that human beings do not need traditional medicine.

Below, I will list some types of deaths and the symptoms they can generate in the current body:

Burned at the Stake

This death is caused by combustion. This was the type of death given to those accused of treason, religious crimes, heresy, or witchcraft. While it is true that this type of execution was used by Native Americans, the Byzantine Empire, and in ancient India, in my sessions I have witnessed execution for witchcraft in greater numbers.

Let's remember that in ancient times anything that had no logical explanation was understood to be witchcraft or the work of the devil. Thus, many healers who used herbs or their hands, seers who predicted the future, and mediums who could see and communicate with spirits were accused of being heretics and witches and burned alive. Later we will see how this type of murder has affected the feminine energy of the person.

Let's try to imagine for a moment what the person being burned might feel. We could start by thinking about what happens to the skin when it is touched by fire, continuing through the muscles and then the bones. To this, let us add what the lungs can feel as they contract and burn, the lack of air, the sensation as if the heart was going to explode, the blurred vision due to the smoke and the smell of one's own body burning; and we would still have to talk about the emotional and mental experience. Death at the stake is one of the most traumatic. People who in trance returned to a life where they were burned alive not only reported all of the above but also described how their soul began to detach from their body in an attempt not to feel, while they watched from above how their body was consumed.

So, what kind of symptoms can be found in people who experienced this type of death in another life? The answer can be varied, but I will mention the ones I heard from the mouths of my own clients:

- Respiratory problems, such as asthma or the constant feeling of having a closed throat.

- Skin problems, such as birthmarks, allergies, psoriasis or eczema. I have seen clients whose skin on their hands peels and hurts in stressful situations.
- Joint problems.
- Muscle problems.
- Fear of public speaking.

Falls

The trauma of death from a fall is associated both with the impact of the body on the surface and with everything that is thought while the body is falling. Obviously, there are people who may die from a slip resulting in a blow to the head, but the most traumatic are those where the person fell into a ravine or off a cliff, regardless of whether this was related to suicide, accident, or execution.

Imagine what a body falling into a cliff with rocks at the bottom can feel like. The impact breaks the bones, spine, and spinal cord. On the other hand, there is the brain and what it can feel when it impacts and bursts.

This type of death can trigger the following conditions:

- Fibromyalgia.
- Emotional, mental, and energetic disconnection of the head from the rest of the body.
- Spinal column problems.
- Mobility problems in general.
- Fear of heights.

Within this type of death, I have seen people with problems walking, unexplained pain throughout the body, and muscle atrophy.

If the death by fall was the result of an act of suicide, then it would be elementary to understand what was going through the suicidal person's mind before jumping. This will be related to the way he/she feels in the current life.

Poisoning

In this category we find death by poisons and toxic substances such as stings, bites, inhalation of gases, overdose, and anesthesia among others.

Depending on the type of poisoning, the body may fall asleep before it dies, as occurs with anesthesia, some gases, or an overdose. If the body is unconscious before death, it can cause great confusion to the soul when it detaches from the body since it will not understand what is happening.

As for sting and bite poisoning, the poison travels through the blood causing different symptoms during the agony that leads to death. In the case of poisons that are ingested, let us think about the path it takes: the taste that is felt in the mouth, as well as what the throat, esophagus, and stomach feel as it moves along its path.

Although this does not make sense to us, death by poisoning leaves a kind of aftermath or symptom in the soul at the energetic level, which will be brought or transferred to the current body. So, what kind of symptoms can people who died under these circumstances present?

- Respiratory problems.
- Digestive problems.
- Skin marks in the area of the sting or bite.
- Disconnection or numbness.
- Confused state.
- Numbness.
- Drowsiness

If the poisoning was provoked by someone else, either by an enemy, derived from a betrayal, or from an execution, imagine all that can be thought during the agony of the body, in case it is conscious. In addition to the physical pains, others will also be experienced on an emotional level that can lead the victim to utter timeless phrases that complicate the entrapment of the soul. I will discuss these timeless phrases, transcendence, and consequences in the next chapter.

In one of the Past Life Therapy sessions I facilitated in a workshop on Soul Entrapment and Soul Retrieval in Lima (Peru), a patient showed an unexplained swelling of the tongue and reported that she was experiencing an almost permanent state of confusion that did not allow her to follow through with her life plans.

Once in a trance state, while we were working around the symptom related to the tongue, the patient returned to a past life where she was about to be sacrificed for religious purposes. The sacrifice consisted of tearing out her tongue, so I asked her to relive that moment more deeply. To my surprise, she told me everything that was being done to her, assuring me that she felt nothing. It was at that moment that I suspected that perhaps she had been given a pre-sacrifice beverage. When I asked her the question, she confirmed it. She had been given a drink containing seeds and roots, which had numbed her. In this life she still felt that confusion because of the concoction.

Buried Alive

We don't have to go far back in time to find cases in which people were buried alive when they were presumed dead. The writer Luis Zapata de Chaves (1526 - 1595) relates in his work *Varia Historia* some cases of premature and accidental burial during the plague that hit Spain in the 16th century, where some people were taken for dead, when in fact they were not, and were thrown into the common grave with the other corpses, then had lime poured over them.

Even in the present time we can find in the news cases in which a person, supposedly dead, woke up during their own wake to the astonishment of the attendants. Cases have also been reported in which screams were heard coming from the grave and in which it was discovered, once the coffin was opened, that the person had been alive and had tried to get out, noting scratches in the wood and the absence of fingernails.

In ancient times being buried alive was due to a lack of scientific methods and current equipment to detect the pulse or brain waves, thinking that the person had died when in fact he was suffering from catalepsy, a disorder that produces a state of body stiffness and lack of stimuli as happens with a deceased person. All this is caused by a nervous disorder.

We can also find in the history of mankind cases in which burial alive was a type of execution. In ancient Rome, a *vestal virgin* was buried alive when she violated her vows of celibacy. On the other hand, in medieval Italy, murderers were buried alive. In feudal Russia, women who had murdered their husbands were put in a well.

Of course, there are also cases in which a person was buried alive as a result of an accident, an attack, or a natural disaster. This may be the case of miners trapped in collapsed mines or people trapped in the rubble of buildings collapsed by an earthquake or bombing.

No matter the reason a person has died from being buried alive, the reality is that most will have the same conditions:

- Claustrophobia
- Choking sensation
- Anxiety
- The feeling of being dead while alive
- Drowsiness
- The feeling of not being heard

These symptoms will be present at a subconscious level and will be triggered when facing scenarios in which they are locked in. This could occur when being in an elevator, an airplane, a dark room, the subway, etc.

Hanging

Hanging causes death by mechanical asphyxiation and suffocation. The best-known cases of this type of death are those related to hanging, which renders the individual unconscious due to lack of air, causing convulsive movements, and producing a rapid death. What actually produces death is *ischemia*, cellular stress caused by any transient or permanent decrease in blood flow.

While dying by hanging may be related to suicide, this type of death is more commonly known as a type of execution. In Salem, for example, a small village in Massachusetts, during February 1692 to 1693, nineteen people were hanged on charges of witchcraft. In Spain, hanging was the most common method of execution until 1832. In England, death by hanging was introduced by the Anglo-Saxon tribes, and by the 18th century hanging had become the main form of punishment for capital crimes. Hanging is still used as a legal method of execution in some countries in Asia and Africa, such as Afghanistan, Bangladesh, Botswana, India, Iran, Iraq, Japan, Kuwait, Malaysia, Nigeria, the Palestinian Authority, South Sudan, and Sudan.

What does the body experience during this type of death?
- Closure of the carotid arteries resulting in cerebral hypoxia
- Closure of the jugular veins
- Rupture of the neck, resulting in traumatic spinal cord injury or even involuntary decapitation
- Closure of the airway

The types of symptoms that people killed by hanging may present in their current life include:
- Neck pain
- Difficulty breathing
- Feeling of disconnection between the head and the rest of the body (emotions or sensations)
- Discomfort when using anything around the neck
- Fear and anxiety of public speaking
- Spine problems
- Problems in the spine

When the person has suffered this type of death in past lives, it is very important to ask them to reestablish the connection of the head with the rest of the body and of the head with the heart—all of this in order to end the possible disconnection they may feel.

Decapitation

This death is caused by the separation of the head from the rest of the body, which generates massive bleeding and a decrease in blood pressure. All of this leads to a loss of consciousness and brain death. One of the debates regarding this type of death revolves around whether death is instantaneous due to the massive blood loss that leads to loss of consciousness. Scientific evidence indicates that, after decapitation, about 13 seconds of consciousness are available. This time is the amount of high-energy phosphates that the cytochromes in the brain have available to maintain it without oxygen or glucose.

Decapitation can be by axe, guillotine, sword, and even due to certain types of accidents. In France, after the revolution, it was used to execute the condemned. In Japan, decapitation was given as the second part of *Seppuku* or suicide by unraveling, to end the agony of the suicide.

The symptoms of those who died from decapitation can be very similar to those who died by hanging, with the difference that in these cases the energetic disconnection between the head and the rest of the body could be felt more intensely. These are some phrases that my clients, who had such a death in a previous life, expressed during the interview prior to their hypnosis session:

- "I feel disconnected."
- "I don't feel present."
- "I can think love, but I can't feel it."
- "I have difficulty swallowing."
- "I feel weakness in my neck area."

These phrases become more relevant when the person indicates that there is no logical or medical explanation for what they are experiencing. This is what makes me suspect that these sensations may be coming from another experience, from another life. Without even realizing it, the person may be indicating to me the reason they are having these symptoms.

As with the hanging, the goal of the session is to allow the patient to reconnect the head with the trunk, to allow them to feel again.

Suicide

We must begin by explaining that with suicide it is the body that dies, not the spirit, and that it is this spirit in possible depression and bitterness that will continue to experience all that it experienced before taking its own life. In other words, suicide will not end the suffering that led them to make that decision.

What I have noticed in these sessions is that even after the death of the body, the spirit is still immersed in the virtual reality that it created, that is, in its own darkness. That is why many are slow to realize what has happened, and for that reason, do not get to see the light or those beings of light that come to their aid. In the book *Nosso Lar* by Chico Xavier, we can find the description given by the spirit of André Luiz about an intermediate place between the earthly plane and the light where the spirits that for some reason or another are lost can be found. André relates how he himself was accused of suicide for having incurred in excesses that ended with the deterioration of his body.

In the *The Spirits' Book* by Allan Kardec, we can find a whole section on the weariness of life, suicide, from which I will share the following segment that will give us a better explanation of what was explained above.

> 950. What is to be thought of those who take their own life in the hope of arriving sooner at a better life? "Another folly! Let them do good and they will be surer to reach such a state. Their suicide will only delay their entrance into a better world, and they themselves will ask to come back in order to complete the life that they cut short through a wrong-headed idea. A wrong, no matter what it may be, never opens the sanctuary of the elect to anyone."

I have been able to confirm this through people who in a past life had committed suicide. The first thing they experienced was being in darkness for a long time and seeing no one coming to help them. Something else I noticed was that the same lessons that had been left over were carried over into the current life with the aggravating factor that this time they seemed to be even more complicated and the challenges greater.

I still remember the case of a young woman in her early twenties who came to me in one of my first practice sessions, who already at her young age had had to face all kinds of challenges and setbacks. When she returned to the past life where all this had originated for her soul, we were able to realize that, when she was very young, she experienced the death of her parents, which led her to feel a great emptiness, loneliness, and a total lack of meaning in life. This situation caused her to take her own life by slitting her wrists.

What I learned early on in my hypnosis practice is that there is really no escape from the lessons we must learn. Whether we turn our backs on them, avoid them, or decide to end our lives with the idea of closure, the truth is that nothing ends. Those lessons will follow us into another life, another body.

Another thing I noticed was that some had suicidal tendencies in their current life because they had committed suicide in a previous life. As my teacher José Luis Cabouli told me, "Death does not make anyone a saint," that is to say that death does not solve any problem for us.

A person who has died under these circumstances in a past life could have the following symptoms:

- Suicidal tendencies
- Lack of interest in life
- The feeling of being plunged into darkness
- The feeling of being confused or lost
- The feeling of being victims

In short, there are many conditions that can occur, but it is also key to know the phrases that I have heard from my clients during the interview prior to a session:

- "I feel immersed in total darkness."
- "I feel like I'm lost, and I don't know where to go."
- "I wish this would all be over now."
- "I didn't want to be born."
- "This is all too much for me."

The Wheat Field

Zoe scheduled an Introspective Hypnosis session to work on several symptoms, including a stomach condition that prevented her from eating much, an allergy to wheat, and an unexplained pain in her throat that caused her to cough frequently. Already in a hypnotic trance state and after a few minutes of therapy, I asked her to look for the next transcendental event that her soul needed to work on.

Antonio: Five, four, three, two, one. You are already there. In that place, is it day or night? What's going on and what are you feeling?

Zoe: I think it's daytime.

A: What's going on?

Z: I don't know. I don't see anything.

A: No problem. You don't need to see, just feel your body and your emotions. What are you experiencing?

Z: I feel my body.

A: Okay. What do you feel in your body, is there any part that feels different?

Z: Yes, pain in my throat.

A: Very good! Feel that pain deeper in your throat. Does that ache feel like what's happening to your throat?

Z: Like someone is choking me.

A: That's right. It feels deeper like you're being choked. I'm going to count from three to one, and you'll go to the moment when you're being choked. Three, two, one. You're already there. What's happening?

Z: I can't breathe! [She exclaimed, shaking his head from side to side with a pained expression.] I can't breathe.

A: What's going on, who's choking you?

Z: My sister is choking me.

A: How old are you there?

Z: 20 years old.

A: And what's your name?

Z: Mary [she answered, confirming that it was a past life event].

A: Why is your sister choking you?

Z: She is choking me because we had an argument. She is jealous of me.

A: And, while she is choking you, what else is going on?

Z: I'm telling her to let me go, to let go of my throat [she said to me as she moved as if trying to get loose from someone] I'm going to die.

A: Feel that. Allow your body to experience that fully. What is your sister telling you?

Z: She is telling me that she is jealous of me because her boyfriend is in love with me. She is jealous of me and doesn't want me to live.

A: Fast forward a little more. What's going on?

Z: She doesn't want to let me go. She's choking me because she wants to kill me. I can't breathe! I smell like fire. I smell smoke all around me.

A: Where do you think you are? What place is that?

Z: I don't know. I'm on the grass. There's grass burning. There's a lot of grass on fire, and I'm there. I feel like I'm suffocating.

A: Is your sister still with you?

Z: No, she left. I'm alone and there's a lot of smoke around. I'm lying on the grass and I can't move because I can't breathe. There is a lot of grass or grain. I think it's wheat. There is very tall wheat all around me.

After this conversation it was easy for me to figure out the origin of her sore throat and cough in her current life and also her wheat allergy. Now I had to find out what else had happened in this young woman's life to cause her soul to be trapped in this experience and create Zoe's symptoms.

A: What else is going on?

Z: I can't breathe [she replied in a soft, agonized voice].

A: And so far what would you say has been the most difficult moment of this experience?

Z: When I'm suffocating.

A: Okay. I'm going to count from three to one, and when I get to one, you'll go back to the moment when you're suffocating. Allow your body to feel everything more intensely. Three, two, one. You are suffocating now.

Z: The smoke is in my throat! I'm choking!

A: And what are your physical reactions while you are suffocating?

Z: I can't breathe. I'm coughing. I'm having trouble breathing.

A: And while you can't breathe, what are your emotional reactions?

Z: I am sad.

A: What are your emotional reactions?

Z: I'm sad with all this smoke around [she said regretfully]. And with the wheat so high and abundant, there's no way to get out. I can't get out.

A: While that's going on, what are you thinking about?

Z: That I'm dying. I'm going to die because there's no way out of here. I can't see the road. I can only see the sky, the grass, and the smoke in the grass.

A: How is all this affecting you in your life as Zoe when you can't breathe, you feel sad, and you think you are going to die? All those feelings, what do they make you do?

Z: My life is choking me too. I feel like I can't speak, I can't speak my truth. I can't say what I think.

A: And when you can't speak your truth, what does it prevent you from doing?

Z: I don't want to hurt people. I don't want to tell them exactly what I think.

A: Now, I want you to go to the moment when that body dies. Feel that fire, the wheat, and the smoke. You're already there. What's happening?

Z: I can't breathe anymore [she said, coughing]. There's no more oxygen.

A: And while you can't breathe, how does the stomach feel?

Z: My stomach and throat are on fire. I'm lying on the grass in the smoke, and I'm dying. I can't breathe. I'm suffocating [she explained in a softer voice].

This is how I assisted Zoe through the dying process of that body, asking her the necessary questions to make her aware that that body had died and that none of it would affect her anymore.

That woman's body had died because of the fire in the wheat field, which had ended up suffocating her and causing her to feel burning in her throat and stomach. A few months after that session, I contacted Zoe and she told me that the symptom had completely disappeared and that she could now eat food that she had never been able to before.

Thrown From a Balcony

Sophia came in for an Introspective Hypnosis session to deal with some emotional situations she was going through. When I saw her enter my office, I noticed that she was walking slowly and very carefully, as if she did not have a good balance.

Among the physical problems she mentioned during our initial interview was a chronic back pain that she had been experiencing for a little over two decades. That was the reason she had difficulty walking and getting up after sitting for a while. She had visited a doctor on a few occasions, but he had found nothing to justify what she was feeling. However, the pain was still there.

Already in a trance, Sophia visited a past life in which she was a slave girl of African descent who, along with her mother, worked in the house of a plantation owner. It was through this man that she experienced all kinds of abuse and was exposed to very sad circumstances. When I asked her to go to the next key scene of that reincarnation, she went to when she was already a young married woman who had been freed from slavery.

Her husband was an alcoholic and constantly abused her. As she related to me the arguments she had with him and his aggressiveness, I could see the look of terror on her face. When I asked her where she was, she told me she was on a balcony or terrace.

Sophia: I fell from a balcony [she said with a pained expression on her face].

Antonio: How old are you there?

S: Thirty.

A: How did that happen?

S: Someone pushed me.

A: What's going on while you're being pushed?

S: I'm screaming.

A: While you are falling?

S: Yes [she answered as she groaned in pain].

A: What is happening?

S: I hit the ground.

A: And while that is happening, what are your physical reactions? What is happening to your physical body?

S: It is broken.

A: And while your body is broken, what are your emotional reactions at that moment?

S: None.

A: And what are your mental reactions while your body is broken and you feel no emotions?

S: I am going to die. I am going to die.

A: How does this affect you in your life as Sophia? All these sensations, what do they make you do?

S: Feel pain.

A: And what does that pain stop you from doing in your life as Sophia?

S: Walking. It hurts when I walk.

We had found the origin of her back pain and walking problems in her current body. Now, I had to help her close that chapter, to release some of the energy that had been trapped in that event, not having processed the death of her body correctly.

A: Let's see how this experience begins. I'm going to count from three to one, and I want you to go to the moment when you are being pushed. Notice who is pushing you. Three, two, one. You're already there. What's happening before you get pushed?

S: It's my husband! [she said in surprise].

A: Why is he pushing you?

S: He's drunk [shaking her head from side to side].

A: So what else is going on?

S: He's telling me I'm a good-for-nothing.

A: Why is he telling you that?

S: I tried to prepare dinner, but I couldn't. I'm sick.

A: Do you have children?

S: No.

A: What is happening now?

S: I'm sick [she answered as she began to breathe rapidly]. And he's holding me down.

A: What happens next?

S: He's shaking me.

A: What happens next?

S: He's telling me I'm worthless. He's pushing me! Oh, God!

A: I'm going to count from three to one and you'll go back to the instant he's pushing you, but this time let your body feel everything it needs to feel to end this thing for good. Three, two, one. You are already there. What is happening?

S: Oh, God! I am dying.

A: Have you fallen on the floor?

S: Yes.

A: I'm going to count from three to one, and when I get to one, I'll touch your forehead and you'll feel the moment you hit with more intensity. Three, two, one. Feel that.

S: Oh, God! [she screamed and shook her head from side to side] .My back is killing me.

A: And while your back is killing you, how does your spine feel?

S: It hurts!

A: And while your spine hurts, what do your lungs feel like?

S: They are collapsing.

A: And while that's taking place, what does your heart feel like?

S: It's... it's... [The pain was so severe that she could not finish the description of what she felt.]

A: And while that is taking place, what is your brain feeling?

S: It's scared!

A: What's the last thought you have in that brain?

S: He killed me!

A: Now move to the instant you leave your body, understanding that with the death of that body this experience is over forever and nothing is going to affect you.

The session continued for a few more minutes as we evaluated the lessons to be learned in that life and visited others looking for the origin of other ailments.

At the conclusion of the experience, I gave her a few minutes to re-engage as it had been intense and we had worked on several of her emotions. When Sophia finally recovered, I saw on her face an expression of amazement and joy at the same time. The pain in her back was completely gone.

S: Look! I can get up without pain. I can put on my shoes without any problems. I've had that pain for twenty years, and I don't have it anymore.

Sophia's soul, going through an emotional situation similar to the one she experienced in the life of the young woman thrown from the balcony, not only remembered what had happened in that life but also recreated the pain she suffered in that body, causing her for many years the ailments she brought to the session.

Having guided people back to the origin of their symptoms for many years, I can conclude two things: most cases are associated with the death of the body in a previous life; and by helping them relive the experience and allowing them to feel what they felt at the time, the symptoms disappear. Hypnotherapists Aurelio Mejia and Jose Luis Cabouli have witnessed the same in their sessions. That is why, in the courses I teach, I always tell my students that in order to heal, we must feel. Psychology maintains the same concept when seeking to desensitize a trauma.

The Harassed Sailor

Joseph scheduled an Introspective Hypnosis session with the motivation to find the origin of the symptoms he had been experiencing since childhood. One of them was the need to tear off pieces of his skin, a disorder known as dermatillomania, and the other was the insomnia he had suffered since he was very young. In addition, he was very uncomfortable with the marks he had on his body, especially on his face, as they embarrassed him when he was at his place of work.

During the interview, while he was telling me about his life, I tried to find some traumatic event that could have triggered these conditions, but Joseph only remembered having a happy childhood.

While in hypnotic trance, as we were following the symptoms he had mentioned to me, he got to an event in his childhood where he was with his parents in the car and he was drawing something on a piece of paper. As his father saw that the ink from the pen was staining his hands and clothes, he asked his mother to throw the paper out the window. This had caused Joseph a lot of sadness and frustration, that in a moment of happiness someone would tear away the thing that made him happy and throw it away. Joseph felt this was unfair as he was not doing anything wrong.

This was somehow an event that made him react to something he had experienced previously in another life. Something that for an adult might be so simple, for Joseph as a child, had awakened a subconscious memory.

Antonio: Where do you feel that sadness when you see the paper and pen rolling on the floor?

Joseph: In the chest [he answered crying].

A: And what does it feel like in the chest, like what's happening to the chest?

J: More like I feel it in my head now. It feels like a pressure.

A: Like what's happening to the head? Like what?

J: Like it's being squeezed.

A: That's it. I'm going to count from three to one, and you're going to go to the first moment you feel that pressure in your head. Three, two, one. If you knew, where are you now while they're pressing on your head?

J: Like on a ship. I'm a sailor and I'm arguing with someone [he said breaking into tears].

A: And if you knew, what is this argument about?

J: I don't know. Like differences.

A: That's it, go on. Feel everything you have to feel.

J: They're slapping me around, like starting a fight.

A: That's it, a little more. Keep going.

J: I feel like I'm defending something.

A: The first thing that comes to your mind. If you knew, what is it that you're defending?

J: It's for something unfair!

This was exactly what he had felt when his parents threw his drawing out the car window.

A: What is it that you are defending? Tell me the first thing that comes to your mind.

J: My dignity.

A: That's right. And so far what has been the most difficult moment of that experience on the ship?

J: Protecting my life.

A: And in that moment when you're protecting your life, what are your physical reactions?

J: The urge to protect my space, to not have my space invaded. I want to avoid being trampled on, mistreated.

A: And in that instant, what are your emotional reactions?

J: Anger, but it is not an anger of hatred, but of being trampled on.

A: And when you feel that anger, what are your mental reactions?

J: Screaming, raising my voice, saying 'this is it' and that I am not going to allow this.

A: Now I want you to see how all this 'I have an urge to protect my space, my dignity, to not be trampled on, to not be mistreated, to feel anger, to want to scream, to raise my voice and say enough is enough' is affecting your life as Joseph. What does it make you do in your life as Joseph?

J: I lock myself in my home, but I'm also very afraid to scream and reclaim my dignity. A lot of times I keep quiet. It's something I'd like to do in my work [referring to his present life] but I feel like I'm being trampled on.

A: And what does this stop you from doing?

J: Talking, making decisions.

A: Now I'm going to count from three to one, and I want you to go to the next important event on that ship in the life of that sailor who is defending himself. Allow your body to feel everything it needs to feel to complete this experience. Three, two, one. If you knew, what's happening now?

J: I want to do my work and they won't let me. They invade me, they bother me, they don't want me. I don't mess with anyone and I keep doing my job [he said, crying].

A: What do they tell you? Repeat what they tell you when they pick on you.

J: I can't say exactly, but they point at me a lot and make fun of me.

A: What do you feel when they point and tease you?

J: I feel like I want to ignore them and get on with my work, but they are getting on my nerves.

A: Go a little further ahead and see what happens. Three, two, one. What's happening now?

J: They conspire and talk to each other. They get together. They're good together, and they don't want me there. Why don't they want me? I don't know, I can't pinpoint it. Even he [one of the sailors] can't pinpoint why he's here.

A: That's it. Go on.

J: He doesn't understand [he said through tears]. There is no escape because we are in the middle of the sea. I move to another side and they are there. I can't let them out of my sight. I look for my space, I look to be alone and I can't. I enjoy it for a short time. I enjoy it for a short time. There are two of them, specifically two that are glued together, that look as if they were one [he continued, covering his face with his hands]. They're old, they have long hair.

A: Move forward to the next important event. Three, two, one. You're already there. If you knew, what's going on now?

J: I'm like in a cabin on that wooden boat, man. I'm in a wide space and I'm sitting down. They're at the door. It's a stalking. They stand there at the door. I'm just sitting and looking at them, but there's no words. It's a form of harassment.

A: I'm going to count from three to one and I want you to fast forward to when something happens. Three, two, one. You're already there, what's happening?

J: I move to the front of the boat, grab like a gun that was there, grab it, point it at them and shoot one, the one on the left.

A: So what happens now?

J: I don't know, I don't kind of sense it.

A: I want you to move to the last moment of that life, see how it ends. Three, two, one. You're already there.

J: I jumped off the boat! I dropped the gun and jumped.

A: So what happens now that you're in the water?

J: I'm swimming, staying afloat, watching the boat pass in front of me. Even though I jumped in, I have a sense of release. Even though I jumped into the open sea and what awaits me is death, I feel free because I'm in the sea and there's nothing around me. I get sunburned [he said, crying].

A: What happens to your body when the sun burns it?

J: My face!

A: That's right. What happens to your face?

J: It starts to feel hot and toasty. It burns my skin. That's where I stay, and that's where I died [he said, crying inconsolably].

A: And up to this point, what has been the most difficult moment of that experience at sea?

J: Tolerating the physical because, emotionally, I was not affected because I had freed myself, because I had made a decision.

A: And at this moment when you tolerate the physical abuse, what are your physical reactions there?

J: I only see my face. I'm looking at myself from above, looking up at the sky, looking for air. I feel my body, from the neck down, as if I am floating. My body is submerged in the water, only my face is looking up, trying not to sink.

A: And at that moment, what are your emotional reactions?

J: There are not many emotions, I just have the feeling of being free, of not being in that place, it is beyond what is happening physically, of being in a place where death is certain. It's a matter of days, but it was worth it.

A: And at that point, what are your mental reactions?

J: It was just worth it.

A: Now I want you to see how all this not feeling from the neck down, not having any emotion, just being free and that it was worth it, is affecting your life as Joseph. What does all this make you do?

J: That boat is my job [referring to his job in this life], and I'm afraid to make that decision and I keep holding on.

A: What decision is that?

J: To leave, to throw myself off that boat. I'm holding on in that scenario where I'm being followed and harassed.

A: And this fear of making decisions, the scenario of being followed and harassed, what does that stop you from doing in your life as Joseph?

J: It keeps me from being free, it takes away my rest. I have to take medication to be able to rest. I am lacerated, my self-esteem is lacerated.

The session continued for a few more minutes. We helped the sailor to complete all that he had not been able to do in this life, to become aware of all that had happened while his body was dying. I asked him to talk to those men who had harassed him to get back his energy, his peace, and his sleep, as it was also harming Joseph's life, manifesting itself as insomnia.

We were also able to find the link to his skin problems in his current life with the wounds created by the sun as his body floated. When I asked him to visit the event of that death one more time, he was able to notice that, as the body floated, there was a disconnection of the head with the rest of the body.

Finally, we can see how this death, which we could consider a suicide as a result of extreme stress and survival, had not solved anything. The sailor made this decision to escape the situation in which he found himself. He himself said that even though he knew that what awaited him was death, he longed for his freedom. In life today, Joseph was experiencing a similar situation by relating his job to the ship and to the same harassment he suffered today to the harassment he suffered in the seaman's life.

Death had solved nothing, for it is the physical body that dies, but it is the soul that continues with the unfinished lessons. It is the soul that remains trapped in that experience, causing it to feel in the present body everything it felt at that time.

Perhaps the sailor's symptoms were triggered in Joseph during the event with his parents in the car, the one in which he felt trampled, invaded, and invalidated.

The Sleeping Woman Inside the Coffin

During the Soul Entrapment and Soul Retrieval workshop I taught in early 2021, Galina, a workshop attendee and Introspective Hypnosis practitioner, was drawn for one of three Past Life Therapy demonstration sessions. During the short interview we had before the session began, I asked her what she thought her soul needed to heal that day. Her response was, "to get people to understand my message because I am always misunderstood. For example, when I am in my doctor's office and I try to explain that I feel dead inside, he tells me that I look normal. I can't get people to listen to me," she said in tears.

This is one of the typical cases in which the symptoms have no logical explanation. The doctors even told her that they had not found anything and that what she was perceiving was coming from her head. The latter made Galina feel sad and condemned to live with that feeling.

Below, I share part of the dialogue of the session:

Antonio: I want you to go to one of those moments when you are trying to send your message across and people don't understand what you are trying to tell them because you feel dead inside. What is going on in that memory?

Galina: I'm in the doctor's office and my whole body hurts. My muscles ache and I've started gaining weight, and I can't understand what's happening to me. I'm falling asleep [she told me as she cried]. I'm just falling asleep. I'm so weak I can't move around my apartment. My whole body hurts.

A: Feel that in your body. Feel that your body hurts.

G: I sleep all day. I have no energy. The doctors say it's in my head, but it's not. Something is wrong. I have to crawl around in my apartment, and I can't get out of bed. I started getting rashes and my whole body itches. I feel like my whole body is giving up. Something is wrong!

A: So now I want you to feel your body tired, feel your body weak. Feel that you are falling asleep, that you are in pain. And as you focus on that, what are you feeling in your body right now?

G: I am in a coffin! Let me out! Let me out! Let me out! I'm alive!

A: Go on...

G: I can't breathe! Let me out! Let me out! I want to live!

By following the symptoms and asking her questions about them and asking her to feel them more intensely, we had created a bridge between the present life and the experience in which her soul was trapped. Galina had returned to a past life in which she had apparently been buried alive. Now, it was up to her to find out what had happened to help her soul end that entrapment.

A: Go on a little longer, what happens next?

G: I think I'm dead. I can breathe now.

A: I'm going to count from three to one, and I want you to go to the beginning of this experience to understand how it starts before you get to that coffin, even before that. Three, two, one. You're already there. How does this experience start?

G: I hear the nails. They are closing the coffin. I can hear them, but I don't say anything. Maybe I'm asleep.

A: Go on.

G: It's like being in a dream and then waking up. I'm so sleepy. I fell asleep and they thought I died? I don't know.

A: It doesn't matter. Go on...

G: I feel like the coffin is moving. It's moving down, but I feel like I'm sleeping, like I'm being rocked.

A: Is your body male or female?

G: I don't know.

A: It doesn't matter. Continue...

G: The coffin being lowered, and I feel like it's rocking. That makes me sleep and it feels good. I don't understand where I am.

A: Go on...

G: It stops. It stops moving.

A: Continue a little more...

G: I start to feel the lack of oxygen. I'm shivering. I think it's cold, very cold [she described, bursting into tears]. It's so cold and dark! Let me out! I don't want to die!

A: So far, what has been the most difficult moment of this experience?

G: When they don't listen to me [referring to the symptom she had mentioned during the interview].

A: And while they don't listen to you, what are your physical reactions?

G: It is cold, so cold.

A: And while you feel cold, what are your emotional reactions?

G: I don't want to die!

A: And while you feel cold and don't want to die, what are your mental reactions?

G: I can't breathe!

A: Now I want you to see how all this is affecting your life as Galina. When you feel cold, when you don't want to die, when you can't breathe, and they can't hear you, what does it make you do in your life as Galina?

G: I have problems with my thyroid. My extremities are cold all the time.

A: And what does this stop you from doing?

G: I don't know [in a very low tone of voice, as if she was falling asleep].

A: I'm going to count from three to one, and I want you to go to the beginning of all this. How does this all start, even before anything happened to you? Allow your body to experience everything it needs to experience and your soul to do whatever it needs to do to end this experience forever. Three, two, one. You're already there. How does this all start?

G: I am a woman, and I have a husband and children. I am happy because I have a lot of love and affection. I love them and they love me.

A: Go on. What else is happening?

G: I think I have an illness, but I don't know what kind. I feel weak sometimes, and I lie down to gain strength [she said, with difficulty breathing].

A: A little more. What happens next?

G: They take care of me. My children and husband are worried because it happens all the time. I lie down and sleep, then I get my strength back and I'm fine. They love me so much!

A: Keep going. Fast forward a little more to the moment when something happens. Three, two, one. You're already there.

G: I fell asleep. I'm tired, very tired. I'm young, but my body is so exhausted that I fall asleep.

A: Alright, just sleep. Now, move forward to the moment when you wake up. Three, two, one.

G: I'm in the coffin! [she uttered, trembling and crying desperately].

So far, we had been able to find out how this young woman had ended up buried alive, the product of a rare disease that made her feel very weak, forcing her to sleep. When I asked her to come forward when she woke up, she was already in the coffin. This can only lead us to suppose that her family thought she had died and that is why they buried her.

What remained for us now was to help her soul to become aware of that death in order to end her entrapment and symptoms.

A: Allow your body to feel everything more intensely. Listen to the nails.

G: Why? I'm alive!

A: What are your legs feeling while that is happening?

G: I'm so cold!

A: Feel your arms, what are they feeling? Feel your chest and lungs. What are your lungs feeling?

G: I'm so cold! [she cried, shivering, and rubbing her hands together]. "I don't want to die!"

A: Feel your throat. What is your throat feeling? What is your heart feeling?

G: I don't want to die! I am gasping for breath. My heart is beating too fast. I want to live!

A: What is the last thought you are able to think in that brain?

G: They didn't listen to me.

A: When you are ready, let that body die. Leave that body understanding that with the death of that body that experience is over forever, and none of it belongs to you anymore. Now, talk to your family. What do you want to tell them?

G: I love them so much. I'm sorry I left, but I was so tired. You didn't know. It's not your fault. I forgive you and don't blame yourselves for my death.

Next, I asked the young woman to collect her energy from that body, to unite it with her soul by bringing it into the light. We had solved the mystery of her symptoms. Her soul had been trapped in that life where she was buried alive, where she could not process her death completely and correctly out of desperation to make herself heard to be taken out of the coffin because she was alive.

A few days later I contacted Galina to follow up with her to let me know how she felt after the session. She told me that during the time of the interview she told me about the symptoms she had been having in 2013 without knowing why she was doing so, symptoms she did not have at the present time. How was this possible?

It seems that Galina was already in full regression while I was asking her this question. Her soul, which does not understand time, had brought her back to that memory in 2013 because she knew there was something pending. It was that memory that triggered what happened in the rest of her session.

Galina told me that she now had more energy and that even her body temperature had changed because her limbs were no longer cold.

This is an excerpt from the message she wrote to me:

Antonio, you have opened something in me, you have been able to literally touch my soul! I have no other explanation. It's beautiful!

It's powerful! It's soul healing! It was simply magical and I thank you for it from the bottom of my heart!

The feeling that people no longer listen to me disappeared. My hands and toes no longer feel frozen.

The Innocent Maid

Martha came to my office with a desire to experience a past life regression. During our initial dialogue she told me about a discomfort she had in her neck for as long as she could remember. The discomfort was so great that it would not allow her to wear anything around her neck.

Immediately, the description of her symptom made me suspect that it was coming from another body, but I did not mention it to her as this might make her nervous and affect the process.

During the hypnotic regression I gradually took her back in time to a younger age, then to her childhood and from there to the time when she was in her mother's womb, a stage from which we obtained a lot of information and answers. Next, I instructed her to visualize a kind of time tunnel, which she went through as I counted. At the end of this process, Martha was already in another life.

Antonio: Look at your feet and tell me what you're wearing.

Martha: Black shoes with straps, like a girl's shoes.

A: Very good. Now, see what you're wearing.

M: A dress, an apron, and I have white socks.

A: What color is your skin?

M: White.

A: What color is your hair?

M: Blond.

A: Is your body young or adult? Is it male or female?

M: Young. Female.

A: See if you have any ornaments on your arms or head.

M: On my head I have something. I think it's a hat.

A: What color is it?

M: White.

A: And your apron?

M: White.

A: Look around you. What do you see?

M: A lot of people. It's like an old time, long dresses and hats.

A: How do you feel there?

M: Afraid.

A: Why are you afraid?

M: I don't know [she answered timidly], but I am afraid.

A: Keep walking and tell me everything you see around you.

M: It's a square with a lot of people around, as if they were watching something. I'm there walking. I see something made of wood.

A: And that wooden thing, what does it look like? Are the people around that wooden thing?

M: Yeah. It's like when they're going to sacrifice or hang somebody.

Up to this point, Martha had no idea what she was seeing, but I already suspected what was going to happen and what she was about to experience.

A: Do you see someone in that wooden thing or not?

M: There are two people. They are two men.

A: Pay attention, what are people saying?

M: 'Poor thing, she doesn't deserve that.' [She began to cry, as if she was already realizing what was going on.]

A: And how do you feel when you see that?

M: Scared [she said, crying deeply as her breath hitched]. I'm so scared!

A: Are they going to do something to you, or is it someone else?

M: To me [she said, surprised and crying].

A: Have you done anything to make them do that to you?

M: No, I haven't done anything!

A: What are they accusing you of?

M: I don't know!

A: Let's find out. Let's go back to the moment when you are caught or accused.

When Martha stepped back to the moment she was arrested, she told me that she was in a large house and that a lady in a black dress was accusing her of something. When I asked her to look the woman in the eyes and tell me if she had ever seen those eyes in her current life, she tearfully replied that they were those of her sister-in-law, with whom she happened to have had many problems.

The woman had accused her of stealing jewelry from her when in fact she had not. Martha worked as a maid in that house and her name in that life was Maria, and at the time she was seventeen years old. Maria (Martha) told me that when someone was accused, they were sentenced to hang, and in this case the lady was very powerful.

I asked Maria to move forward a little further. When she did, she began to tell me that a man with his face covered apprehended her and took her away with her hands tied, informing her that she was going to be hanged.

A: Go ahead until the moment they are in the wooden structure. What are they going to do there?

M: They are putting the noose around my neck. I'm very scared. People cry a lot because I'm young. They hang me and leave me there alone [she said, crying inconsolably].

A: Move to the moment you get out of the body. There is no more suffering. Now that you are out of the body, what do you see below? Are you floating?

M: Yes, I see the gathered people walking, but I am calm. I feel no pain, no fear.

A: Do you realize that death is an illusion? Now, if we assess the life that has ended, what do you think you should have learned from it?

M: To defend myself, to be stronger.

A: And do you think you passed the test?

M: No.

A: I'll ask you another question, were you by any chance supposed to learn about forgiveness?

M: Yes.

A: Did you forgive?

M: No.

Mary had not forgiven those who had unjustly accused and killed her. Moreover, by being hanged feeling fear and rage, she could not process the death of that body correctly, without fully feeling that experience on a physical, emotional, and mental level. That is why her soul remained imprisoned in that event, feeling that death over and over again.

The Healer's Heart

In September 2020 I invited Victoria to one of the mentoring meetings with practitioners taking the Introspective Hypnosis course. On that occasion I wanted to do a demonstration using Victoria as a volunteer. I knew that she had had a conversation with her family about her mediumship that had left her very upset, and I knew that this would be an ideal opportunity for her to heal.

Another teaching I wanted to share that day was that a hypnotic induction was not necessary to bring a person to an expanded state of consciousness. This approach in the sessions is the one that generates great amazement in everyone who attends the workshops I give on Past Life Therapy and Soul Entrapment. I also had the same reaction when I attended one of José Luis Cabouli's workshops.

How is it possible for someone to enter a trance without an induction? First, we must remember that when the person brings a symptom that has no logical or medical explanation, we assume that it comes from a traumatic experience excluded from the conscious mind. That is, we do not remember it. The traumatic experience may have taken place a few months ago, in infancy, in the womb, or even in a past life. The only thing conscious for the person is the symptom, which would be the tip of the iceberg, while the traumatic event is hidden at the base.

Now, if the symptom comes from a past experience, then the past is not the past, but is here and now in the form of that symptom. That is why we define therapeutic work as helping the person to make conscious what is unconscious, by following the symptom and asking the necessary questions to direct them to the traumatic experience that originated it. We have already mentioned that the soul does not understand time, so we could say that the person is here (in the present) but is also in the traumatic experience (in what we call the past). That is why, in the session, a kind of bridge can be built to take them to the origin of the symptom. During this process we help the person enter into an expanded state of consciousness, also called trance.

But how is it possible to enter a trance state without the need for an induction? When the person is taught to feel the symptom they have in their body, asking them to describe that sensation, pain or discomfort, and then asking them to associate it with something familiar, it is at that moment that they begin to access the information they have in their subconscious, thus gaining access to the experience that originated it. The more the person is helped to make conscious what is felt in the body, the deeper the therapeutic work will be and therefore the deeper the hypnotic trance and the result will be.

In reality, when a person is with closed eyes visiting past memories, they are already in regression. We must understand that the trance is progressive, that is, as we continue to ask the person questions about that experience, they will gradually enter into hypnotic trance without even realizing it, disassociating themselves from the here and now.

I will now relate the conversation I had with Victoria during her session:

Antonio: Remember that conversation with them. And while you remember it, tell me what you are feeling.

Victoria: Hurt, sadness.

A: And while you are feeling hurt and sad, where in your body do you experience that?

V: In my heart [she answered in tears].

A: Okay, feel that. Allow yourself to feel that pain and sadness in your heart. And tell me, that feeling in your heart, feels like what? What kind of feeling is it?

V: Like my heart is about to stop.

A: Let's intensify that now. One, make it more intense now. Two, more intense. Three, even more intense. Now, I'm going to count from three to one, and you're going to go to the instant you feel like your heart is about to stop. Three, two, one. You're already there.

Victoria went to that moment, her body arched as if she couldn't breathe normally, as if she was about to go into cardiac arrest.

A: What's happening now? If you knew, even if you think you're imagining it, where are you, what's happening?

V: I can feel my heart beating.

A: In that place where you are, do you have the body of a man or a woman?

V: A woman's.

A: Young or old?

V: Middle-aged.

A: What place is that?

V: It seems to be a forest. I'm standing.

A: Why does your heart feel this way?

V: I don't know. I was walking around looking for something, and I started having pain, like a needle was going into my heart, into my chest. It feels heavy.

A: What do you do at that moment?

V: I try to sit up and ask for help, but I don't think they can hear me.

A: Move forward a little more. What else is going on?

V: I'm lying there looking at the sky and I feel like this is the end, but I don't want to leave.

A: Why don't you want to leave?

V: My children! [she exclaimed, crying].

A: How many children do you have?

V: Three.

A: What else is going on?

V: I don't know.

A: Go ahead and see what's going on.

V: I see someone approaching, but I don't think it's a person. It's a light, a very intense light.

A: Let's ask that light to wait a moment for you. So far, what has been the most difficult moment of this experience?

V: Letting go, letting go.

A: I'm going to count from three to one, and let's see how this all starts. I want you to go to the moment before you went to the forest, to the moment when this experience begins. Three, two, one. You are already there. Where are you now?

V: I'm at home with my kids. I'm getting ready to go out, and I'm asking them to be quiet and behave. I'm getting my basket of medicine ready. I am walking to the door.

A: Before you walk out that door, I want you to look those children in the eye and tell me if you have seen them anywhere else.

V: It's my grandmother [she said, crying with emotion]. Also, my nephew and my mother.

A: What happens after you are about to leave?

V: My heart feels very heavy, but I know I have to go meet someone who needs my help.

A: How do you help people?

V: I heal them with things I prepare from nature. Also with my hands.

A: What is in your hands?

V: It is a beautiful and powerful energy that I feel every time I go to help someone.

A: Okay, go on. You are going to help this person and what happens?

V: I am walking and I can hear nature. My throat is dry. As I'm trying to drink water, I feel a very strong pain in my heart, like I'm being stabbed.

A: Let yourself feel that even more. What is happening now?

V: I'm trying to massage my chest [she said with difficulty breathing]. I'm trying to see if I can help myself.

A: And while that is happening, what are your physical reactions?

V: My arm and hands are getting numb.

A: And what are your emotional reactions?

V: I feel anxious.

A: And while you are feeling anxious there, what are your mental reactions?

V: Sadness and self-doubt.

A: How is all this affecting you in your life as Victoria? As you feel your arms and hands going numb, you experience anxiety, and you think about that sadness and those doubts, what is all that making you do in your life as Victoria?

V: I have panic attacks, and I doubt myself too much.

A: And all of this, what does it prevent you from doing?

V: Being who I'm supposed to be one hundred percent.

A: I'm going to count from three to one, and when I get to one, you're going to feel your heart stop. Let your body live this experience again. Three, two, one. You are already there. What are you feeling?

V: I can't breathe [she answered as her body arched, showing signs of great pain in her chest].

A: What do your lungs feel like?

V: They feel clogged, constricted.

A: How does your throat feel?

V: Very dry.

A: What is the last thought you get to have in that brain?

V: Why am I leaving my children alone? [she said, crying inconsolably].

A: And when you ask yourself why you are leaving your children alone, what does this make you do in Victoria's life?

V: Be overprotective.

A: And what does this prevent you from doing?

V: Allowing my children to make their own decisions [crying even more deeply].

A: That's right, very good. Move to the moment when your body dies. Allow your body to die, understanding that with the death of that body that experience is over forever, and none of this is going to affect you anymore.

As you float there, I want you to go and find your children. Explain to them what happened, that it is your time to go, that they will be fine, and that you will be watching over them. Tell them whatever you want to tell them.

V: It's my time to go, but I love them so much. They will be okay because Mom will be taking care of you every day. I will help you be who you really are. I love you.

A: And as you say goodbye to them, what do you think you had to learn in that life?

V: That I'm not in control, especially of what goes on around me.

A: Did you learn that lesson?

V: I don't think so.

A: What happens when you don't learn a lesson?

V: I have to repeat it.

A: So you're going to come back as Victoria. How is she going to deal with the same situation? Through whom?

V: Through her family members.

A: So, what can you tell her about that? Because, apparently, it's still affecting her.

V: It's okay. You don't have to be in control of everything all the time. What they think of you doesn't make you who you really are.

So, it was this way that Victoria's spirit detached from the body she had, created healing in that woman's life, continued to counsel her, then said goodbye and departed into the light. The incident with her family had triggered a psychosomatic symptom that was associated with the moment of death of the other body, which she had not been able to process satisfactorily.

The situation, in a way, was the same: the pain in the heart and the sadness of her heart were related to having to move away from her loved ones and understanding that she could not be in control.

THE PERISPIRIT AND BIRTHMARKS

The Perispirit

According to spiritist science, the term *perispirit* comes from the Greek word *peri* meaning around and the Latin *spiritus* meaning soul. It is used to refer to a kind of semi-material envelope that surrounds the spirit, which serves as a link between the spirit and the body. At death, the physical body is destroyed (decomposed) leaving only the perispirit, which would become the ethereal body of the spirit. This body is usually invisible to us, but there are occasions when it can become visible and even tangible.

According to *The Spirits' Book* by Allan Kardec, the perispirit is the vaporous substance that covers the spirits. They draw it from the universal fluid of each globe (planet). That is why it is not the same in all worlds; it is as if they change their clothing according to the planet where they are. Spirits not only reincarnate on Earth, but we can also reincarnate on other planets in the universe.

Now, the physical body is the instrument through which the soul perceives pain. The pain that the soul may experience is not actually physical pain, but is merely a memory of the pain that body felt. To better understand this concept, let's think of those people who have suffered the amputation of a limb and who, despite no longer having it, continue to experience a supposed pain coming from it. So, is it the missing limb that is causing the pain, or is it the memory or impression of that limb registered in the brain that is causing it? In the same way, the perispirit is the agent of the external sensations channeled by the organs of the body, but when the body dies and the disconnection of the soul from the body is finalized, these sensations become generalized since they are not subject to specific organs. It could be said that the perispirit behaves as a nervous fluid between the body and the spirit.

Birthmarks

Birthmarks are abnormalities that occur on the skin of newborns. They can be vascular or pigmented. The former are red because they are formed by blood vessels that did not develop properly, while the pigmented ones are formed by a group of skin-colored cells. Their origin is unknown. Some come from the family clan, some disappear with time and others remain.

There are different beliefs about them. Some societies have attributed them to bad luck, while for others it means the complete opposite. Most birthmarks are benign and may provide more information than we think.

***

Based on the explanation of the perispirit and birthmarks, along with what was developed in the previous chapter regarding the symptoms associated with different types of deaths, we can conclude that the after-effects of these deaths are not only imprinted on the soul and perispirit, but can also be transmitted to the physical body that the soul currently inhabits. It seems that in some way when the soul reincarnates it is already surrounded by the perispirit that stores the pain and physical traumas it obtained from previous bodies, transferring part of that imprint to the present body. That is why on some occasions this manifests itself visually through birthmarks. This rule does not apply in one hundred percent of cases, but it has happened enough times to establish this relationship.

It is known that children tend to remember their most recent past life more easily because the memory is still fresh in them. As they grow up, their parents, religion, society and culture block those memories until they are completely forgotten. Canadian doctor Ian Stevenson, head of the department of psychiatry at Virginia University, in his book *Where Reincarnation and Biology Intersect* presented 2,600 cases of children who remembered their past lives. These were children from Buddhist and Hindu countries in South Asia. Of these cases, 65 were thoroughly documented by him, and he found that the information provided was consistent with where they lived, their family, and how they had died. The symptoms presented by these people and the birthmarks were related to the way in which their body had died, especially if their deaths had been violent.

Something that has happened many times during hypnosis sessions is that, when the person returns to a past life, red marks appear on the body just before visiting the scene of death. These marks are usually associated with the type of injury to the body that caused the death. In the time I have been practicing spiritual hypnosis I have learned to monitor the body of my clients while they are in hypnotic trance, as it can provide very rich information.

On my YouTube channel, Antonio Sangio, there is a case (number 144) of a young middle-aged client, who seconds before I asked her to go forward to the last moment of that past life, showed a large red spot around her neck. This spot was so obvious that she even pointed her finger so that whoever was watching that video would pay attention to it. A few seconds later, she described to me how in that life she died by hanging. Apparently all that is registered in the perispirit can manifest not only as psychosomatic symptoms, birth marks, but also when a traumatic death is visited while in an expanded or altered state of consciousness (trance).

Based on the explanation about the symptoms according to the types of death, as from the explanation about the perispirit and birthmarks, one could believe that the symptoms we bring from past visits could only be associated to the type of death and the agony of the body when this is not so. While it is true that there may be karma accumulated in a past life that must be settled in the present life, following the principle of action and reaction, in the next chapter we will see how the phrases or commands we pronounced at crucial moments in our past lives may also generate symptoms. Many times, these will be the reason for the entrapment of our soul or for being trapped in the role of victim.

TIMELESS PHRASES

We have previously said that the soul does not understand time and that for it, everything happens now. We have also explained that for the soul, life is only one life with experiences in different bodies. That is to say, the soul never dies and perfects itself in each reincarnation. It is coincidentally the timelessness of the soul that causes its entrapment in a past experience when it has not been fully processed, when something was left pending or unfinished. But what other situations can cause soul entrapment? Promises, vows, pacts, oaths, curses and even what we pronounce or think before we die.

All these timeless phrases mentioned above have something in common: energy, intention, and above all, that they are pronounced by our soul and not by the body we had in that life. But how so? If the body we had when we said that sentence has already died, what difference does it make? Wouldn't what was said remain without effect? Well no, and it is explained by the very fact that the soul does not understand time and that for it, everything is happening now. What was said while occupying other bodies is still valid. The point is that we do not remember it consciously, but we carry it on a subconscious level, and we already know that the subconscious is anchored to the soul and goes beyond the existence of the physical body. It does not matter that the body is another, male or female, or that the context of the current life has nothing to do with that past life.

This was one of the concepts I learned from hypnotherapist José Luis Cabouli during my training in Past Life Therapy, which transformed my therapeutic approach. He helped me pay attention to these timeless phrases in order to relate them to the symptom my clients bring to their session and help them not only to understand the origin of the symptom, but also to reverse that which their soul had pronounced.

In my hypnosis sessions, I have had clients who were having problems maintaining or making a sexual or emotional commitment and others who were having problems with money. They returned to past lives where they had been priests or nuns, or where they had made a promise of eternal love, to name a few examples. The priest and the nun still carried with them the vows of poverty and chastity, even though in this life they even had a different gender. The woman who made a promise of eternal love in her past life was still waiting for her beloved from that life, causing her not to make her commitment to the partners she had in the current life.

The word is energy and vibration. When it is projected with a specific intention, the results can be positive, but when we do not understand the magnitude of what we are saying and projecting, when we do not put a time limit to what we are projecting, many times the consequences can be disastrous.

Promises

A promise is anything that a person commits to perform out of his or her own free will or for favors received. Promises, as I mentioned earlier, carry the energy and will of the person. Here are some examples:

- Promises of love
- Promises to parents
- Promises to children
- Promises to religious figures
- Promises to God

The list could be longer, but this allows us to have an idea about them. Examples of promises can be:

- "I will love you forever."
- "You will be my only love."
- "I will wait for you forever."
- "I will never stop watching over you."
- "I give my life in exchange for making you happy."

None of these examples has a timeline or expiration. What will happen then to the one who swore eternal love? Well, not only will they love that person during their past life in which they pronounced the promise, but they will continue to do so in the next reincarnation regardless of whether their beloved spirit is incarnated or not. Even worse if the promise was also "I will wait for you forever," for that is exactly what they will do. In a next reincarnation, the individual will feel that he is waiting for a loved one who never arrives, and as a consequence they will reject any further commitment, feeling that by accepting they would be failing to keep their promise.

The promises "I will wait for you forever" and "I will never stop watching over you" could even cause *post mortem* entrapment. This means that the spirit, once that life is over, decides not to go to the light and rather stay to wait for the loved one or simply to watch over them.

Vows

We will refer basically to the religious vows, also known as monastic or canonical vows, which distinguish the religious from the laity. These are three:

- Vow of poverty
- Vow of obedience
- Vow of chastity

The religious seek to be poor, obedient to his or her superiors and to preserve his or her chastity in order to imitate Christ. With these vows, the objective is to have access to spiritual salvation through renouncing earthly pleasures, as Christ did.

By renouncing earthly pleasures, the soul will carry the same premise with it to its next reincarnation, causing it to behave in the same way. On a subconscious level, the spirit will feel that it should not have acquisitions or material possessions, causing a kind of self-sabotage, an unconscious and uncontrollable behavior that will block its financial prosperity or acquisition of goods. In the same way, the vow of chastity can generate inconveniences when trying to maintain a love relationship or when having sexual intercourse, because the soul will feel that it is failing to fulfill this vow.

I have witnessed how these vows also produce confusion, depression, and sadness when not being able to understand the reason or the origin of their problems.

If we are talking about vows, it is essential to also mention the marriage vows that take place within the Catholic religion, as these can affect the soul. It may not be a vow that transcends other bodies, but it will affect both people in the current life. This is a common example of a marriage vow:

Groom: I, (groom's name), take you, (bride's name), to be my wife. And I give myself to you and promise to be faithful to you in joy and in sorrow, in sickness and in health all the days of my life.

Bride: I, (name of bride), love you, (name of groom), as my husband. And I give myself to you and promise to be faithful to you in joy and in sorrow, in sickness and in health all the days of my life.

The spouses are pledging to be faithful to each other at all times, "all the days of their lives." And, not only that. The priest also pronounces the following as he presents the wedding rings:

"May the Lord bless these rings that you are about to give to each other as a sign of love and fidelity."

In those rings, there is the intention and energy of what is being pronounced. This would be sealing the marriage vow, but the priest still pronounces something else:

"What God has joined together, let no man put asunder."

From the point of view of the timelessness of the soul, what is the soul committing itself to at this point? Assuming that the soul understands that the vow is in effect during the physical life of the body, this vow will be in effect regardless of whether the marriage between these people works out or not, whether they later divorce or not. How many times have we seen divorced people trying to rebuild their lives with other partners over and over again, still feeling tied to the first husband or wife? It is not a rule, but it does happen.

Pacts

From the Latin *pactum*, a pact is an alliance, agreement, deal, or commitment in which those involved agree to respect what is stipulated. What was agreed upon will not only affect us if the pact was made in this life, but we also bring with us those made in previous lives.

During past life regressions, generally there have been found pacts with cults, also known as 'pacts with darkness', carried out during rituals. In some cases, these pacts were signed with blood, carrying our energy in it and sealing the deal. It does not matter if the person is in another life, in a totally different context, or uninterested in these types of cults. These dark forces will generate all kinds of problems trying to force the soul to comply with the pact.

Oaths

Some consider a promise and an oath to be the same thing. The difference lies in the fact that with oaths there is a witness to ensure the fulfillment of the commitment. An oath can be sworn by a divine power, by another person, institution, or even by the Bible:

- "I swear on my mother that…"
- "I swear to God that…"
- "I swear on my father's ashes that I will take revenge."

Curses

A curse is a wish for something bad to happen to a person or persons. While I use the word *wish*, we are actually projecting our energy and part of our consciousness against another person while wishing them harm.

Usually, the curse begins with the words "I wish". Here are some samples:

- "May you burn in hell."
- "May you suffer as you have made me suffer."

- "May you and your offspring be plunged into poverty."
- "May you die."

When we curse the energy of hatred, anger, or resentment projected onto others will return to us, affecting us in the same way. From a spiritual point of view, where it is said that we all come to learn from love, compassion, and understanding that we are all one, cursing goes against all those principles. Whether in a past life or a current one, the negative energy that we once projected onto others will come back to us, and in most cases, in the form of misfortune and bad luck.

The Last Thought

Although the soul can pronounce timeless phrases at any time, whether in a past incarnation or in the current one, I believe that those having the most influence and can present themselves as symptoms in our next reincarnation are the ones we say or think at the time of death, during the agony of our body. If in past lives our demise occurred at the stake, on the gallows, or with a previous torture, what could we have thought or said during our last minutes of life? Phrases like:

- "Damn you all."
- "May you all rot in hell."
- "I will follow you for eternity until I get my revenge."
- "May you suffer as you have made me suffer."

In the case of those who had special gifts, such as healers, seers and mediums, and those accused as witches and hanged or burned alive, the phrases they may have pronounced in their mind are:

- "Healing is dangerous."
- "It is not good to activate my gifts."
- "Using my hands can get me killed."

If on the other hand we were the aggressors, whether we have tortured, raped, or killed someone, we may at the moment of our death become aware of what we did and regret it. Phrases we may think during our agony could be:

- "I don't deserve God's forgiveness."
- "I will not have enough lives to pay off my debt."
- "I do not deserve happiness."
- "I will not stop until I repair the damage I have done".

Everything we think or say during the agony of our body in a past life, will be immediately converted into a kind of pattern that will be activated and that the soul will take with it to future reincarnations, causing problems, symptoms, and a great confusion because it does not understand the reason for its behavior.

Those who cursed will be affected by the energy of their own projected evil intentions. Those who swore vengeance may keep their spirit on this plane seeking revenge on their tormentors, causing them to become a lost soul.

Those healers accused of witchcraft and executed will unconsciously block their gifts in the next reincarnation. More than once I have worked with mediums who did not want to accept their gift in this life and tried to block it or deny the mission they had been given. All this generated great fear and depression in them. In this life, even though they were not accused of anything, they felt that manifesting or developing their gifts was dangerous.

The aggressors in past lives, when thinking or pronouncing phrases where they said they did not deserve forgiveness or to be happy, will automatically pass from the role of aggressor to that of victim, entering a circle of self-sabotage in their next reincarnations. They will feel that they do not deserve to be happy or to be forgiven and will attract situations that make them feel exactly that way.

The Symptom

When a person comes to a hypnosis session seeking help, they do not come saying, "I need to break a promise I made in a past life," or "I need to end my role as a victim," or "I need to break the vows I made when I was a priest." What the person will bring with them will be symptoms, whether physical, mental or emotional.

For example, the one who died by hanging in public will perhaps arrive saying that they have impediments to speak in public, that their body becomes tense, that they feel a lump in their throat, that they feel that spectators are judging them, and that at that moment they feel rage against them.

The aggressor who died regretful and said, "I don't deserve forgiveness or to be happy," will more than likely tell me during his interview about the unhappy life he has lived since birth, including abusive relationships with his partners, causing him low self-esteem and lack of self-love.

Healers or mediums accused and judged by witches will come to session asking me to help them block those gifts because it causes them so much fear and stress. No matter how much I explain to them the importance of that gift in helping others, they will be closed to any explanation and will react the same way they reacted when they were accused.

In my practice of hypnosis I learned to pay attention to these symptoms not only during the session, but from the beginning of the interview. There will be times when during the pre-session interview they will tell me, "I feel like I don't deserve to be happy," or "I feel like I have a black cloud over me all the time," or "I feel persecuted all the time." Without realizing what they are doing, they will give me the key to what is really going on with them because many times the phrase they pronounce comes from the experience in which their soul was trapped.

The Therapeutic Approach

Once the symptom is detected, hypnotherapists help the person to make conscious what for them is unconscious at that moment. It is not a matter of going back in time and space, for the person has the symptom here and now. Then by asking the necessary questions about the symptom, we build the bridge that will lead us to the experience where it originated. The symptom will become the thread that will lead the person to the root. It usually directs us to a past life. Next we need to understand what happened, the story of that life and specifically at what time that phrase was pronounced and what exactly that phrase contained. All this will lead us to understand the origin of the symptom and the behavior that is affecting the person now.

In the case of a promise, oath, or pact, the same person will have to indicate that this is left without effect. In the case of a curse, it is recommended to ask for forgiveness for what was said and for the negative intentions, and then express that the curse is without effect. As for what was mentioned in the previous paragraph as well as for the last thing we think before dying, it is necessary to determine how what we pronounced or thought is affecting us in our current life. This can be found through two questions: What does this make you do in your life as (current name)? What does this prevent you from doing in your life as (current name)?

After asking these questions it is key that at the time of the death of the body they are helped to become aware that with the death of that body that experience is over forever. With this, what is sought is to disconnect them from that experience and end the entrapment. Of course for this purpose it is necessary that the soul completes all that it could not do at that moment.

The Curse of the Healer

During the Healing the Wounded Feminine workshop I facilitated in November 2021, Caroline, a Jamaican woman in her sixties, volunteered for one of the demonstration sessions of the Past Life Therapy technique. When I asked her what her soul needed to heal, her response was immediate: "I have abandonment issues. I am short of breath and suffer from anxiety and skin problems, mostly itching, dryness, and cancer." She had experienced abandonment at various times in her life, starting with her mother when she was three years old, continuing with her father who had remained emotionally disconnected from her, and finally her partners who had also been emotionally disconnected.

Antonio: Take a deep breath and close your eyes. And while you do that, I want you to think about all the symptoms you have mentioned to me: the shortness of breath, the feeling anxious. Allow your body to feel all that more intensely [I said, noticing how Caroline was quickly becoming emotional]. What do you feel when you can't breathe, when you are short of breath?

Caroline: I feel very emotional.

A: That's right, feel emotional more intensely. And, when you feel emotional and you can't breathe, what else do you experience in your body?

C: I feel it in my throat more intensely.

A: And if you know, it's like what's going on with your throat?

C: It's a lot of fear that is closing my throat.

A: I'm going to count from three to one, and I want you to go to that moment when you feel the fear closing your throat. Three, two, one. You are already there. If you knew, even if you think you're making it up, where are you as you feel that fear closing your throat that won't let you breathe?

C: It's dark. There's a lot of smoke in the air.

A: That's right. What else is going on?

C: They're burning women at the stake! [she cried, bursting into tears]. I'm scared, but I'm not running. I don't know why I'm not running.

A: That's right, where are you now?

C: I don't know, in a horrible, dark place.

A: That's it, smell that smoke and those women's skin burning. Continue. What else is going on?

C: I just feel confused. I feel like I know some of the women and I want to support them, that's why I'm there.

A: That's it, go on. What happens next?

C: I feel like I want to cry. [She burst into tears again.]

A: Go ahead and cry. Go on.

C: What's going on?

C: Someone I know from this life is asking me to go to her, but I can't move [she said desperately, referring to her current life as Caroline].

A: That's it, continue a little more, what's happening now?

C: They are coming for me. They are two soldiers. They're holding me down, and they're tying me to the stake.

A: Go on a little more. What are they doing now?

C: They are lighting the fire, but I can't feel it. I don't feel emotional. I can't feel my body either. [shaking her head from side to side].

Caroline's description gave me to understand that her soul had already started to detach from her body so as not to feel pain.

A: I'm going to count from three to one, and I want you to let your body die. Three, two, one...

C: Why are you doing this to us? We haven't done anything! It's terrible!

A: Let your body die. I'm going to count from three to one, and when I get to one, I want you to go to the beginning of this experience, to the moment when all of this begins for your soul in that life. Allow your body to feel everything it needs to feel. Three, two, one. You are already there. If you knew, how does this begin for your soul in that lifetime?

C: I'm in my cabin and some women come and say, 'Come, you have to come. They are burning. They're burning our friends,' so I run and go. I'm there looking at everything. There's a lot of noise and a lot of people shouting, 'Burn them, they're witches!' It's kind of mass hysteria.

A: Feel all that, continue.

C: I'm confused. I don't understand why this is happening. I am there because of my friends. We work in healing. The men are envious! They are so envious of us!

A: That's right, continue a little more. What happens next?

C: They are taking them to the stake, setting them on fire, and burning them.

A: What has been the most difficult moment of that life so far?

C: Watching my friends being tied up and then set on fire and not being able to do anything to help them.

A: And as you watch your friends go through that, what are your physical reactions?

C: I'm nauseous and I'm having an anxiety attack.

A: And as you experience nausea and an anxiety attack, what are your emotional reactions?

C: I am afraid.

A: And when you are afraid, what are your mental reactions?

C: I am confused.

A: Now I want you to see how all of this is affecting your life as Caroline, when you say you are nauseated, having an anxiety attack, and feeling confused. What does all of this make you do in your life as Caroline?

C: It affects me in many ways. I feel jealous of men. I attract men who want to subjugate me, who want to control me.

A: And when you attract these kinds of men, what does that stop you from doing?

C: I feel anger against men and I react.

A: Alright, now I'm going to count from three to one, and you will go to the moment when they put you on the stake. Three, two, one. You're already there. And, as I count from three to one again, when I get to one you will feel the fire touching your skin and you will feel it more intensely. Three, two, one. Feel that now. What does the skin feel like?

At that moment, Caroline started to sort of convulse and cough, while crying and holding her hands to her neck as if she couldn't breathe.

A: What are the muscles feeling? Feel the muscles, feel the stomach, feel the lungs.

C: My body is going crazy.

A: Feel the throat. What is the throat feeling?

C: My throat is closed and my skin is bristling [she replied, coughing].

A: What does the brain feel when it doesn't get enough oxygen? What is the heart feeling?

Although Caroline could not answer my questions due to crying and coughing, I still sought to help her **become** aware of everything that body had felt in order to end her entrapment.

C: I hate them, I hate them, I hope they die! [she exclaimed while touching her skin as if trying to tear it off]. Oh, my chest hurts!

A: Allow that body to die and get out of it now. Now I want you to talk to them. Tell them they didn't have to kill you and ask them to give you back your energy, the energy they stole from you when they burned you.

C: You bastards, give me my energy back now! You have no right to keep it, give it back to me now.

A: Once you are ready, extend your hand and bring your energy back. Very good! Now I want you to see something else, you told them, 'I hope you die, bastards,' meaning you sent them a curse. When you send a curse, it comes back to you three times stronger. What is that curse causing you?

C: "It prevents me from having a happy and healthy relationship with men," she answered tearfully and without doubting what she was saying.

A: Today you can break that curse, you can free yourself. Do you want to do that?

C: Yes.

A: Then say something like, 'By the power of my own will, today I cancel and cease this curse that I sent to these people. I release them and I release myself.'

C: By my own will, I undo the curse I put on these men, and in doing so I set them free and free myself. I give them back their power.

A: That's right. Now I want you to see where you have been storing the energy of that curse in your body.

C: In my heart, in my lungs, in my throat, in my stomach, and in my power center, also in my shoulders.

A: Then remove that energy from your body, free yourself. What do you think your soul had to learn in that life?

C: Injustice and to be misunderstood. I'm always saying I'm misunderstood.

A: And what lesson comes with the lesson of injustice?

C: The lesson of forgiving others and making sure I am always fair.

That was how, after a few more minutes, Caroline slowly came out of the trance she was in. She had been able to find not only the origin of her physical symptoms, such as shortness of breath and skin problems, but also the root of her pattern of abandonment and always looking for emotionally disconnected men, which prevented her from having a healthy, loving relationship.

Another interesting aspect of the session with Caroline was receiving an email from her the next day in which she thanked me for the session and gave me an update on everything she felt afterward. She also mentioned that she didn't remember cursing the men, which according to me she had clearly heard during her session. Otherwise then, why did she respond so confidently about what the supposed curse she had cast had generated in her? This was a bit confusing.

To be sure, I decided to listen to the recording of the session and clearly heard again, "I hope you die," but it wasn't until I was transcribing the session for inclusion in the present book that I realized that she hadn't actually said that phrase. So where did it come from? Why did I hear it? Why did she immediately respond to something she hadn't actually said?

A few days later I contacted her again to confirm that she had not actually said that curse and that she did not know why I had heard it. This is what she replied to me via email:

Thank you, Antonio. I thank you very much for taking the time to confirm this for me, but I also feel that you have picked up on something that has not been said. There have been times in this life when I have felt like cursing someone, but I have never done so because I understand the karmic repercussion and this life is about being a conduit of light and recognizing divine intent for spiritual evolution in all my experiences, but judging by the intensity of that experience, I have no doubt that I would have cursed them and probably much worse than wishing them death. Blessings, Caroline.

Something I always share in the trainings I lead is what I once read in a book by Michael Newton, that the best therapist for our clients is not us, but their spirit guide, and therefore we must open ourselves to channel their counseling, to let them work through us to help our clients. I am sure this is what happened.

I Will Never Leave You

During one of the workshops on entrapment and retrieval of the soul that I often teach, Leilani was one of the volunteers for one of the demonstration sessions. The main requirement for volunteering was to know what her soul needed to heal. "I can't access my full potential. Every time something good is going to happen, something blocks it," she told me. When I asked her what she felt when she experienced that blockage, she told me a combination of frustration and problems with her hips. "I feel like I can't move," she added.

Without knowing it, Leilani had shared a phrase that came from a parallel experience, from where that symptom had originated. This is a common occurrence during an interview with my clients.

Leilani also told me that, until a couple of months ago, she had felt as if she was going to be paralyzed by her hip problem. From a logical or medical point of view, these discomforts had no explanation. At the beginning of the session, I asked her, as she let her body relax while she was lying down, to think about what she had mentioned.

Antonio: As you feel your heart and your hips, what would you say your hips feel like? Like what's happening to them?

Leilani: Like they are cramping.

A: Okay, experience that more intensely. Feel like they're cramping and feel like you can't move. And if you knew, even if you think you're making it up, where are you while you feel your hips cramped and you can't move?

L: The only thing I can think is that I'm in the car.

A: Okay. So, what's going on in there?

L: I feel like I'm pulling away from something.

A: That's it, keep going a little more.

L: I'm in pain. It's hurting.

A: That's right, where do you feel that pain?

L: In my heart [getting emotional].

A: That's it, feel that pain in your heart more intensely. Continue.

L: It hurts! It's so painful! [she exclaimed in tears].

A: And in that place where you are, do you have a man's body or a woman's body? [trying to find out if it was this life or a past one].

L: A woman's.

A: Go on, why are you going away?

L: Because I want to move on with my life. I don't want to stay stuck.

A: So, what's your name? What do people call you?

L: I think it's just a memory. It's me [referring to a memory from this life].

A: Okay, go on a little bit more. What's happening now?

L: I feel like I'm leaving someone behind and it doesn't feel right. I want that person to come with me, but they don't want to.

A: And if you knew, who is that person you are leaving behind?

L: It's the person I thought was my soulmate.

A: What person is that? What's his name?

L: It's Tom.

A: Okay. What else is going on?

L: I'm starting to feel the pain in my hips, like something is telling me not to leave. 'Don't go, don't go.'

A: That's it, keep going.

L: I want to keep moving forward, but this thing is pulling me back. I don't want to be pulled back, and I want to keep moving forward.

A: And if you knew, what is this thing that is pulling you back?

L: I feel like it's an energy that doesn't want me to leave.

A: Okay. And, what happens next?

L: I'm leaving anyway. It feels like I have something attached to me that doesn't want me to leave.

A: That's it, go on.

L: I don't know what that thing is. I don't know if it's a person or an entity.

Up to this point we had detected that Leilani had begun to feel her hip pain once she got into her car to drive away from the person she considered her soulmate. Even though she was determined to leave, she felt that something was pulling her back to not leave Tom, but she didn't know how to define this which, in a way, tied her to him and made their separation more difficult.

A: So far, what has been the most difficult moment of that experience?

L: The fact that I'm leaving [she told me, crying]. It's painful, but I have to do it. I need to do it for my own sake.

A: And, at this moment when you are leaving for your own good, what are your physical reactions?

L: My heart is about to break. I feel like I'm not going to be able to do anything else without my heart.

A: And at this moment when your heart is about to break, what are your emotional reactions?

L: It's like it's about to burst out of my chest.

A: And what are your mental reactions?

L: That it's okay, that I can do this. I can live without anything holding me back. It's okay, I can do it.

A: Now I want you to see how all this is affecting your life as Leilani, when you say your heart is about to break, your heart is about to burst out of your chest, and you can do it, you can live without this. All that makes you do what?

L: I go on with my life, but I feel empty.

A: And what does that stop you from doing?

L: Being who I really want to be. I feel that there is something that always makes me look back, and I don't want that.

Up to this point we had understood how the separation from Tom had affected her and was still affecting her. That separation was related to her hip pain and not being able to move forward, but there was something that always pulled her back, as if she couldn't quite let go. So, I asked her to back up to the moment when she was saying goodbye to Tom.

A: Fast forward to the moment when you're about to get in the car. Let me know what's going on. Tell me everything you're feeling.

L: I'm very upset with him because I feel like he's let me down. I don't want anything more to do with him. I wish him the best, but I have to go.

A: Then go, and let me know what happens when you leave.

L: It still hurts.

A: Tell me everything you experience as you get in the car.

L: My hips are starting to feel heavier and heavier. I feel like they are losing their balance. I get in the car and have to put a cushion on my hips because the pain is becoming unbearable.

A: A little more, go on.

L: When I sit in the driver's seat and I'm driving, it hurts. I feel like I'm never going to have anything like this again in my life.

We continued to work on that memory, going back to the moment when she had the last conversation with Tom, helping her to say everything she hadn't been able to at the time. Thus, we were able to realize that, in that painful moment, her soul had fragmented and that fragment had stayed in that event, in that timeline. Would this be what was pulling her back and not letting her move forward?

Once I helped Leilani integrate that fragment of her soul with the rest, my intuition told me that the root of the problem was much further back, perhaps in another lifetime.

A: I'm going to count from three to one, and I want you to go backwards and backwards. When you get to one, go to the moment when all this starts for your soul, this feeling like this in your heart and feeling stuck. One, two, three. If you knew, even if you think you're making it up, where are you now?

L: I feel like it's a past life, but I'm not sure.

A: It doesn't matter. You don't have to be sure. Tell me whatever comes to your mind.

L: I feel like I'm a mother.

A: Okay, continue.

L: I feel like I'm telling my child something, but I don't know what.

A: I'm going to count from three to one, and you're going to repeat the first words that come to your mind. Three, two, one. What are you saying to your child?

L: Stay here. You're going to be fine without me, stay here.

A: Once you say those words, what happens next?

L: My son doesn't want me to go, but I'm still going.

A: Okay, go on. Let your body feel everything it needs to feel.

L: I am leaving, but he is crying. My son is crying and I keep looking back telling him it's going to be okay. I'll be right back, you're going to be fine, but he's still crying [she sniffled, covering her eyes].

A: And if you knew, where are you going?

L: I'm going to run some errands.

A: What happens next?

L: I feel that something happened to me. I can't see it, but I feel like I had an accident.

A: That's right. What else is going on?

L: I think my son witnessed that. He's screaming because he saw that I just had an accident and now I'm dead.

A: So far, what has been the most difficult moment of this experience?

L: Hurting my son. I was leaving so I made him suffer.

A: And at this moment when you make your son suffer, what are your physical reactions?

L: My heart hurts, but I need to leave, I need to take charge of my life. I need him to understand that it's okay, but he doesn't understand. And now I had this accident and I feel guilty.

A: And at this time when your heart is hurting and you feel guilty, what are your emotional reactions?

L: I think I shouldn't have left. Maybe I should have stayed with him and maybe I wouldn't have had this accident.

A: What are your mental reactions?

L: I promised him I would never leave again [she said, breaking down in tears]. My soul hurts because I feel like I left.

We had found the phrase that caused Leilani's soul entrapment in that past life. It was about the promise made to her son, a promise that, for her soul, was still valid.

A: Now I want you to see how all this is affecting your life as Leilani, the pain, feeling guilty, believing you shouldn't have left, vowing never to leave again, what is it that makes you do in your life as Leilani?

L: Getting stuck. I want to leave, but I can't because I'm looking back.

A: And what does this stop you from doing?

L: Moving forward.

A: I'm going to count from three to one, and I want you to go back to the moment when you are talking to your son. Allow your body to do whatever it needs to do to complete this experience. Three, two, one. As you are talking to your son, I want you to look into his eyes. Have you seen those eyes before?

L: Yes [she answered, bursting into tears] It's Tom, it's him!"

A: I'm going to count from three to one, and I want you to move forward to the moment when you have the accident. Let your body feel everything it needs to feel more intensely. Three, two, one. You're already there. What's going on? What kind of accident is this?

L: It's something with wheels. It doesn't feel like it's a car, but it has wheels.

A: What's the first part of your body that's affected by that thing with wheels?

L: My hips, oh my God!

We had found the origin of everything Leilani had been feeling from the moment she decided to leave Tom. Why? Because Tom had been her son in that past life, the son who didn't want his mother to leave, the same one who witnessed the accident in which his mother died having been run over and hit in the hips. The mother, who after death promises to never leave him again, to never abandon him again.

But why did Leilani feel the pain in her hips now in her present body? Because as she walked away from Tom in this life, her soul remembered that she had also walked away from him in that past life, and it was that which triggered the pain in her hips. Her soul had made the connection between leaving Tom and the pain in her hip and feeling trapped.

After working with the death event in that life and out of the body, I asked the woman's soul to speak to her son and explain that she needed to go into the light.

A: Explain to your son what just happened to you.

L: I just had an accident. I'm sorry, I'm sorry I left you [she said through tears]. I shouldn't have left you, but now I have to go to the light. I have to go; I have to go because I can't stay here. I love you so much and you're going to be okay. I will come back and we will be together again. I promise you we will be together again.

A: Now I want you to talk to him about the promise you made to him. Tell him, 'Son, I can't keep that promise because I'm going into the light, but you're going to be okay, and you're going to grow up and you're going to experience growing up without me. But I know you can do it.' Tell him whatever you want.

L: I can't come back, but you're going to be okay. You're going to grow and evolve. You don't really need me. You are very powerful on your own. I'm sorry to have to break that promise.

So, after saying goodbye to her son, the woman's spirit (Leilani, in this life) was able to continue on her way to the light.

Once the session was over, Leilani felt very relieved and told me that her hips felt very light. They no longer felt crampy.

I Will Love You Forever

Marcela scheduled a hypnosis session to deal with some issues that prevented her from living peacefully. During the interview she told me about the bad relationship she had had with her mother and the abuse she suffered at the hands of her father. She also told me about a behavior pattern she had detected in her life: every time she had a partner and they were about to formalize their engagement, immediately she would end the relationship. "I can't maintain a serious relationship for long," she told me with confusion and sadness.

Already in a hypnotic state and having visited a memory from her childhood where she had had an altercation with her mother at the age of three, I asked her to go back and look for the event that had generated all this in her life. Below, I share part of the dialogue:

Antonio: Let's see how all this starts, where your soul takes you to teach you the origin of all this, the reason for this pattern. Let your soul go where it has to go. Three, two, one. You are already there. As if you knew, where are you now?

M: I'm Rachel [she said in a calm voice].

A: Rachel, look at your feet, what are you wearing?

M: Some old black leather shoes.

A: What are you wearing?

M: A long black cotton dress.

A: Are you young or old?

M: Young.

A: What color is your skin?

M: White.

A: Look around you, what do you see?

M: Oh, I see it for the first time! [she answered surprised].

A: Who are you seeing?

M: For the first time I see him!

A: Who are you seeing?

M: The soldier!

A: Very good! Tell me about this soldier. How is he dressed?

M: I can't see well, but he's lying under a tree. He has a musket and his hat is on the ground.

A: Is he young or old?

M: 17.

A: Do you know this soldier? Have you seen him before?

M: Oh, he's wounded!

A: Where has he been wounded? Where on his body?

M: He was shot in the stomach and he's bleeding. He's badly wounded. He's an officer.

A: What are you going to do about it?

M: I'm in trouble [she replied in a fearful voice]. I'm not supposed to be around anyone who has anything to do with the war.

A: Who doesn't allow you to do that?

M: Our community, but he is dying.

A: So, what are you going to do about it?

M: I have to help him; I have to help him.

A: Move forward a little bit to see what's going on.

M: I've hidden him in the house, in a place with wood where it will be warmer.

A: Is he saying something to you?

M: He speaks German and can't speak much.

A: Do you speak the same language as him?

M: I heard a little German from my grandmother. But I understand him, I don't know how.

A: Alright, now move forward a little bit to see what's going on with this soldier.

M: He's getting better. I bring him food and keep him hidden, but I can't do it much longer. I'm going to be found out.

A: I want you to move a little further ahead until something else happens. Three, two, one. You're already there. Rachel, what's going on?

M: My family knows I'm hiding him and they don't like that, but they're helping me feed him and telling me this is my responsibility. I'm putting the family in danger.

A: Who tells you that?

M: My mother [she answered in tears].

A: Look at your mother's eyes, have you seen them before?

M: Oh, God! It's Giovanna [referring to her mother in her present life]. I beg her to let me keep him here until he is better. She leaves me because he can't be seen leaving our farm, so I have to do this alone. I feed him and tend to his wounds. He also has broken bones. He is very badly injured. He spends two years in our house.

A: Move forward to the next important event and let's see what happens. Three, two, one. You're already there.

M: He's on horseback and he's out of uniform, since we got rid of him. He's wearing my father's clothes. He's going to leave, and I'm trying to help him escape. I think the war is almost over, but he is not completely safe. Maybe he can escape now.

A: Move forward a little more.

M: I am in love with him, and he is in love with me. I am very young. I'm between 14 or 15 years old.

A: I want you to look the soldier in the eyes. Have you seen those eyes before?

M: Yes, I have. It is Kevin [crying and referring to a partner she had in her current life].

It is relevant to highlight that, when we got to Rachel's life, the first thing Marcela said was that she recognized the wounded soldier, saying that was where she saw him for the first time. How many other times had she seen him? How long had they both been working on lessons at the soul level? What would happen next would give us the answers to life experiences as Marcela.

A: I want you to move back to the moment when you find out whether or not he can escape. Three, two, one. You're already there.

M: We're at the edge of the farm, hiding behind a tree. There's a big fence, and he hands me a spoon. I don't understand. He hands me a silver spoon, and somehow it's a gift to me. It has something engraved on it.

A: What does it say?

M: 'Given this day 1776, I, Arnie Echols, Hessian Officer, give in gratitude to Rachel K. Neal.'

During the writing of this book, I took a moment to look up the meaning of *"Hessian Officer"* and found the following: *Hessian Officers were German soldiers who served as auxiliaries to the British Army during the American War of Independence.*

A: What happens after he gives you that spoon?

M: He hands it to me and kisses me goodbye. I am a young *Quaker* girl, and we can't have anything to do with the war [crying inconsolably].

We are pacifists and peacemakers, and he is a German soldier. If he stays in our community, he will cause great embarrassment to our family. He has to go because he is healthy enough. My family made him leave. I don't know if I'll ever see him again. Oh, God!

The Quakers, also called Friends, belong to a set of historically Christian (Protestant) denominations formally known as the Religious Society of Friends.

A: Move forward to the next important event. Let's see what happens. Three, two, one. You're already there.

M: I'm an old woman and I'm alone.

A: So far, what has been the most difficult moment in Rachel's life?

M: Saying goodbye to him, I loved him so much!

A: I'm going to count from three to one, and I want you to go back to the moment when you are saying goodbye to him. Allow your body to feel whatever it needs to feel and do. Three, two, one. You are already there.

M: My heart is breaking; I miss him so much! I know I'm going to miss him forever [she said crying and shaking her head from side to side]. I still miss him forever.

A: What are your physical reactions as you say goodbye?

M: My heart is breaking and feels empty.

A: And while your heart is breaking and empty, what are your emotional reactions?

M: Feel the loss. I can't do anything to bring him back. I can't change my people, I can't change the war, I can't change all this insanity, this madness. I want my own life, but it is not mine. I belong to a culture where I can't be myself.

A: And how is all this affecting your life as Marcela? When you say, 'I'm heartbroken, I feel the loss, I can't change people, I can't change my life,' what does that make you do in your life as Marcela?

M: It makes me want to help people. I always want to help heal others.

A: What does this prevent you from doing?

M: I feel that love is never mine, just a little bit and then it disappears.

So far, we had the explanation for Marcela's behavior with her partners when she was about to formalize the engagement, but there was more to discover.

We continued to navigate past life as Rachel, helping her through the moment of death of that body as she lay alone in her bed. Her family and friends around her, she felt loved and ready to go. After this, she saw herself floating above her body describing how her body looked like it was asleep and dressed in a Quaker hat.

A: What did you have to learn in that life that just ended?

M: Oh, I felt so much love. I had so much love.

A: Who gave you that love?

M: The soldier. Arnie and I loved each other so much. Not just on the level of the body, but even deeper.

A: Become aware that with the death of that body that experience has ended forever and none of it will affect you anymore. Now, I want you to speak to the soul of that soldier. Tell him that you loved him in that life, and that life is over. I want you to free yourself from the feeling of missing him because later you will be in another body and you will find other partners, and you need to be free.

M: I don't want to be free! I don't want to say goodbye to him.

A: Well, now you understand why in your life as Marcela love never stays, because you don't want to say goodbye to him. This is up to you. You can stay trapped in that life or set your soul free. If you are meant to be together you will find each other again, but you can't close yourself to meeting other men.

M: Okay.

A: Did you make any promises to him?

M: Yes, I did.

A: Go back to that moment when you are making the promise to him. Three, two, one. Go back to that moment again. What are you saying to him?

M: I will miss you and love you forever. I will love you forever and never forget you.

Finally, we had found the missing piece. It was this promise that had her soul trapped in that life, waiting for the soldier, loving him forever, and not forgetting him just as she had promised.

A: Now, do you understand why your soul feels that way, even in your life as Marcela? Do you understand why love doesn't stay? Life as Rachel is over and so is your relationship with him. Now, I want you to explain to him that you can't wait for him forever and you can't love him forever, that you loved him in that body, but that life has ended. Explain that to him.

M: Please, please understand. I have to move on and you have to move on. I loved you so much. Please take that with you, and I will take it with me, but I have to move on to another life.

A: Explain to him that that promise was in that body and in that life, but it is over now.

M: That promise I made to you was in that body and in that life. I have to move on and live another life and love again.

A: Pay attention to what he says to you.

M: He says, 'Thank you. You saved my life, and I will always be grateful. I will always love you, but I am letting you go.'

A: Tell each other that you are now free.

M: Arnie, you are free to love again, and I am free now, too.

We had found the origin of the symptom Marcela brought to the session. Her soul was trapped in Rachel's life with the soldier, the product of a promise of love.

Let us remember that it is not the body but the soul that makes the promise, and that for the soul time does not exist. For Rachel's soul, which is the same as Marcela's, the promise still stood and when the time came to formalize her commitment to other partners in her present life, it was more than likely that her soul felt that she was failing to keep the soldier's promise.

Realizing the consequence of the promise, Rachel (Marcela), agreed to break it, freeing herself and the soldier.

The Witch

During one of the Introspective Hypnosis trainings in the Netherlands, Caroline, who had been experiencing different emotions during the exercises in class, arrived at the last day feeling a headache and a lot of sadness. So severe was her discomfort that she intended to leave the training. I told her to calm down because she was feeling what she was supposed to feel. That last day was dedicated to practices between participants and demonstrations of the technique by me. Because of the latter, I asked her to stay as I knew her discomfort was a result of the spiritual work she had been doing during the previous days. Caroline decided to trust what I had told her and stayed in class waiting for her turn to be part of one of the demonstration sessions, as I had offered. This is what happened after she went into trance:

Antonio: I am going to count from five to one, and you will go to the origin of all that you are feeling. Let your soul feel and do all that is necessary. Five, four, three, two, one. You are already there. Alright, in that place where you are now, is it day or night?

Caroline: I don't know. It's dark.

A: Okay. And, in that darkness, do you feel like you have a body?

C: Yes.

A: Do you feel like you're standing or sitting?

C: I am sitting.

A: And while you are sitting in the dark, does the body feel like a male or a female?

C: Older female.

A: And as you are sitting in this dark place, what are you feeling?

C: Pain.

A: That's right. And as you feel that pain in that darkness and in that body, where are you feeling that pain?

C: In my neck. [Her body began to shudder as if she was about to convulse.]

A: And if you knew, what is causing that pain?

C: I am chained [she said crying].

A: And while you are chained, how does your body feel?

C: In pain.

A: And, while you are feeling that pain, what emotions are you experiencing?

C: I'm sad. [Tears ran down her cheeks.]

A: And while you are feeling sad, what are you thinking about?

C: I am innocent! [she cried more deeply].

A: Why do you think you are chained?

C: Because they are going to kill me.

A: Why are they going to kill you?

C: Because they think I'm a witch.

A: From that place where you are, I'm going to count from three to one, and you're going to go to the moment before you enter that place. Three, two, one. You're already there. Where are you?

C: I'm in a castle.

A: Look at your feet. What are you wearing?

C: Sandals.

A: What are you wearing?

C: White linen.

A: And what are you doing in that castle?

C: I'm in the gardens enjoying myself. The sun is shining and I'm picking herbs.

A: So, what are you doing with those herbs?

C: I put them in a pot.

A: Do you brew something with them?

C: Yes, tea.

A: What do you use that tea for?

C: It's medicine.

A: And what do you use it for?

C: For all kinds of things.

A: Who taught you how to use herbs to make tea?

C: My grandmother.

A: Alright, let's get away from that scene until the moment when someone comes for you. Let's see what happens when they put you in that dark place. [Her body trembled.] Three, two, one. You're already there.

C: They're screaming.

A: Who is screaming?

C: The men from the village.

A: Why are they shouting?

C: They are rounding up the women.

A: Do you know if they are coming for you?

C: Yes [she answered crying].

A: Move to the moment they come for you. Three, two, one. You're already there.

C: They are shouting my name. They have torches with them, fire.

A: What else is going on?

C: They find me in my house.

A: Now, I want you to move to the moment when you're in that dark, lonely place. Three, two, one. What's going on?

C: I'm naked and dirty.

A: Is there anyone else in that place with you?

C: Yes, other women.

A: Do you know what's going to happen to you?

C: They say they're going to hang us, but they're taking as long as they want. We've been here so long. I'm going crazy.

A: Now I want you to move to the moment that body dies. Three, two, one. You're already there.

As soon as I got to number one, her body began to convulse sharply, and her breathing became ragged showing that she was experiencing something traumatic.

A: What is happening?

C: I'm behind a carriage. I'm being dragged.

A: And while you are being dragged, what are you feeling?

C: Pain!

A: Where are you feeling that pain?

C: In my head and in my back [the convulsions continued].

A: And as you experience that pain, what emotions are coming up?

C: Anger.

A: And as you feel that pain and that rage, what are you thinking?

C: I'm going to die.

A: I want you to go to the moment when that body dies. Three, two, one.

C: I have fainted.

A: Is the body alive or dead?

C: Almost dead.

A: While you are passed out, where is your spirit?

C: It's about ten feet above the body.

A: Now move to the moment when you make sure that body is dead.

C: It's already dead.

A: Now that that body is dead, what do you think you were supposed to learn in that life?

C: Pain.

A: How does learning about pain benefit you from a soul point of view?

C: Create empathy.

A: Since you already learned about pain because you already experienced it, don't you think it should be over by now?

C: Yes.

A: Then there is no reason to bring it into this body, Caroline's body. Does it make sense to bring a pain that does not belong to this body?

C: No, but she is in a lot of pain too.

A: So what advice can you give her?

C: To use that empathy with herself. She loves everybody and is empathetic with others, but she has very little self-love.

This is how Caroline got to the root cause of the psychosomatic symptoms she had that had begun to flare up during the days of practice in the Introspective Hypnosis class. The headache and neck pain were related to the agony in the body of the woman who had been unjustly executed.

The sadness and other emotions she felt were also associated with the time she had been locked up without knowing when she would be executed. That is why, during the navigation through that past life, I asked her all the necessary questions so that she could relive the death physically, emotionally, and mentally, finally giving her soul the opportunity to complete everything that had been left unfinished in order to end her entrapment. As I began to bring Caroline out of her hypnotic trance, a different expression could be seen on her face. She looked more cheerful and upbeat. When she finally opened her eyes, she was glowing and let out a few laughs to let us know how good she was feeling.

MASCULINE AND FEMININE ENERGY

Human beings, both men and women, possess these two types of energy. A woman's body channels feminine energy better, while a man's body channels masculine energy more optimally. Think of the representation of yin and yang. In the white section there is a bit of black, and in the black section there is a bit of white.

For our physical, mental, and emotional well-being, it is crucial that these energies are balanced and reconciled, otherwise this imbalance will manifest itself in physical, emotional, or mental symptoms. I learned this concept, as well as the importance of balancing energies, from my teacher Jose Luis Cabouli during the Healing the Wounded Feminine workshop.

Masculine Energy

Represented on the planet by the male body, it is the energy of action, decision, and execution. Think of it as that of the prehistoric hunter who went out to find food for his family or as that of the conqueror. It is also interpreted with strength.

Feminine Energy

Represented on this planet with the female body, it is the energy of creativity and intuition. It is passive and connects us with our soul, essence, and divinity, as it carries with it the mystery of creation. In other words, we could say that it is the energy of the gestation of the universe.

***

Throughout the years, the feminine energy has been relegated by a large part of humanity, which has preferred material goods and earthly desires to that connection with its own essence. It is known that in prehistoric times man recognized this feminine energy and paid tribute to it. Clay figures, sculptures, and drawings have been found in caves where female deities were represented and worshipped.

Later, when man began to work with metals and created the sword, he realized that with it he could conquer other peoples and that he now had the power to decide about life and death. It is at that moment that man began to value strength, power, and control over life more than creation. From worshiping feminine deities, man began to worship warrior gods, thus initiating the supremacy of the masculine energy and the suppression of the feminine and therefore the domination over the woman in whom that energy is represented. We are talking about the existence of thousands of energetically unbalanced generations.

At the beginning of his career José Luis Cabouli, like many of us who practice spiritual hypnosis, was focused on healing trauma, on only treating the origin of the symptom so that it would disappear and his patient would feel relief. Over time he realized that in order to help his patients, this was not enough, but it was also necessary to heal the energies, especially the feminine energy, which is the one that has been suppressed and dominated the most. Not having this energy balanced and reconciled with the masculine energy causes a series of symptoms and behavioral patterns in the affected person.

The invalidation of this energy, and consequently the wounds that arise in it can be generated in the following stages:

- In past lives
- During conception
- During pregnancy

- During birth
- During early childhood

When a person comes to my door seeking help, they do not say, "I need a session to heal my wounded feminine side," or "I need to balance my feminine and masculine energy." The individual comes to the session with symptoms of which they often have no suspicion of their origins. These may be:

- Conflicts with partners
- Difficulty finding the right partner
- Inability to leave abusive relationships
- Fear of becoming pregnant
- Fear of having children
- Difficulty in sexual relationships
- Problems with menstruation
- Blocked creative abilities
- Difficulty expressing and communicating

Although I mention patterns that manifest only when the feminine energy has been wounded or damaged, these can also affect men: first, because men have also had lives as women; and second, because if our mother experienced any of these symptoms while we were in her womb, it could also have affected us. It does not matter whether we currently have a woman's or a man's body.

Next, let's review each of the named stages and the discomforts and/or patterns that may appear in them.

In Past Lives

Many people who have had a session with me returned to lives in which they had been blamed, tortured, and executed. We all know that in the past there were many people accused of being witches or warlocks just for believing or talking about metaphysical subjects. Women who were actually healers and used their hands to heal were accused, out of ignorance, of being witches.

There were also those who had medicinal knowledge of plants and herbs, either in their natural form or as concoctions, not to mention those who had the gift of clairvoyance or mediumship and were accused of having a pact with the devil or darkness.

These people not only kept the trauma of having been unjustly accused, of being in front of a crowd shouting all kinds of insults at them, of having suffered torture and then death, but they also carried with them the nullification of their creative energy with thoughts or decrees like these:

- "Healing is dangerous."
- "I will never use my hands to heal again."
- "Helping others may end my life."
- "They can't know who I really am."

And it doesn't stop there. There are other ways in which this energy was negatively repressed. Just mention the types of torture to which women were subjected in past centuries. We can find artworks that exemplify them, such as The Martyrdom of Saint Agatha by the painter Sebastiano del Piombo, which shows how her breasts are torn off with tongs. As for the torture of women throughout the history of the world, it can be seen that there was a cruelty with the female organs since they represented the creation and carried the secret of life, something that man did not understand and of which it seems he was afraid.

There are other events in past lives that may have damaged the feminine energy, such as the theft of children, rituals that included the sacrifice of children, the loneliness of the woman when her partner or children left for war, the loss of her relatives during the war, and even the abuses committed by officers and soldiers. What kind of command could this generate in the soul and the subconscious?

- "Why have children if they are going to be stolen from me?"
- "Why have children if they can kill them?"
- "Loving children is painful."
- "Being a mother is dangerous."

A few months ago, I had a session with a woman who told me that she didn't have children and that she didn't want to have them either because she felt it was too much responsibility for her. She also felt very sad constantly, with a sense of inexplicable guilt and of not being able to have joy in her life. Once she was in a hypnotic trance and we began to explore the symptoms she had mentioned, the young woman came to a past life where she was very poor, very hungry, and had seven children. At one of the events we visited she tearfully told me that she had lost two of her children and that she did not forgive herself for it. When we arrived at the time of her death, she confirmed that she could never find them and that she felt guilty for not having been able to care for them. She felt that she had failed as a mother. This was the pattern she brought into her current life and the reason for the discomfort she had felt all her life.

During Conception and Pregnancy

In the chapter on soul entrapment, we were able to see how the baby's soul inside the womb can be affected by everything that happens to the mother, such as fears, phobias, emotional conflicts, the place or culture she is in, among other factors. The invalidation of energy, especially feminine energy, begins in the womb. If the mother is in an abusive, unstable relationship or belongs to a society and culture where women are strongly repressed, the soul that occupies the baby's body may not only be trapped in the womb experience, but also the baby's feminine energy will be affected, regardless of whether a boy or a girl is born.

And think about all that the soul of a baby can experience that has been the product of rape, where the mother may not only have been harmed on a physical level but also on an emotional level. The rape may even have caused the fragmentation of the mother's soul. Surely, that little boy or girl will carry with him or her a feeling of rejection, of not being loved, and will have difficulty loving themselves and giving themselves the place they deserve. During the time in their mother's womb, the baby does not know which emotions belong to them and which belong to the mother, because they feel them all as their own. And as I explained earlier, when the baby is born, everything it experienced will be recorded in its subconscious, generating all kinds of symptoms and behavioral patterns.

Is the baby then a victim of this situation? From the point of view of spirituality and reincarnation, the soul that is occupying the baby's body knew beforehand the situation it was going to face and still chose to live it. Remember that we choose our parents before we are born according to what we have to experience through them in the first years of life, in which we are completely vulnerable.

Then the spiritual amnesia to which the baby will be exposed once they are born will turn this circumstance into a real lesson for them. The baby will begin their life being affected by all that they experienced in the womb, and in their evolutionary path they will not only have to learn the why of that situation, but they will also have to learn the opposite of what they experienced from the beginning of their life. Meaning, if they experienced lovelessness, it is more than certain they will have to learn love; if they experienced a lack of connection, it is more than certain they will have to learn to connect with others. But throughout this process of evolution and learning, they will be influenced by the symptoms and behavioral patterns developed during their time in the womb. Here are some examples:

- "No one loves me."
- "It would be better not to have been born."
- "Intimate relationships are dangerous."
- "I feel like I don't own my life."
- "Love does not exist."
- "Why bring children into the world if they only come to suffer?"
- "To be a woman is to be abused."
- "I only have myself."

During Birth and Early Childhood

Nowadays, there are still cultures and societies where greater value is placed on men than on women. This can be seen from the time of birth and early childhood. Girls are taught to do housework and obey their husbands. They learn to cook, clean, embroider and sew, while being groomed to be housewives and pamper their husbands. In some countries, women do not even have the right to education.

Without going too far, in China where the number of children a couple can have is controlled, the majority of babies given up for adoption are female. Faced with a limit on the number of children, parents sometimes choose to keep the male child, who will be able to help work the land or support the family.

From childhood, both boys and girls are programmed, with females generally being the most affected by having their energy disrupted. This leaves emotional wounds that manifest in behavior patterns that limit their creativity and connection to their essence.

From a therapeutic point of view, all this represents a great challenge, especially for those who learn and practice the Introspective Hypnosis technique in countries where females are strongly repressed. Many of the women who come to a session for help find it difficult to understand that victims do not exist, that every painful circumstance holds a lesson, and that we all begin by experiencing the opposite of what we are supposed to learn. Many women find themselves trapped in the role of victim, causing them all kinds of problems. It is not uncommon to hear the following expressions from these types of people:

- "This is what I deserve."
- "My duty is to obey my husband."
- "Everything that happens to me is God's punishment."
- "I must be obedient."
- "I must always support my husband, even if I think he is wrong because he is the breadwinner."
- "Without my husband I will not be able to support myself."

Phrases like these, pronounced during the pre-session interview, may lead us to suspect that the feminine energy is wounded and that the creative part and the connection with her divinity may have been blocked.

During adolescence, there are other circumstances that can also suppress the feminine energy, such as cases of domestic violence and alcoholism. In homes where there is a father who physically or emotionally abuses his wife, it is not only she who is the victim of the situation, but the children as well. The events of terror and panic the children may face during the abuse will not only mark them emotionally and energetically, but may also fragment their soul.

I have seen many of these cases in sessions. For the most part, on an emotional level the girls grow up and end up repeating their mother's behavior pattern. In the case of the men, as they grow up, they often adopt the behavior of their father, whether it be that of a womanizer or even an alcoholic, no matter how much they recognize how much they have suffered because of it. Without being able to understand the reason for their behavior and without being able to control it, they in turn become victims when they see the suffering of their own children, just as they suffered. Men with wounded masculine energy may be heard expressions such as:

- "Men don't cry."
- "Men were born to be in charge."
- "Women are only good for taking care of the house and the children."
- "A real man has more than one woman."
- "In my house I am the boss."
- "This is the way it is because I say so."
- "No woman will leave me."

These expressions not only show a clear disconnection with feminine energy, but also a rejection and repression of it. For the family, this ends up becoming a vicious cycle.

Other traumatic events that damage feminine and masculine energy during childhood are rape and molestation, but I have decided to dedicate an entire chapter to this topic because of its relevance and frequency.

Reconciling Energies

As time has gone by and I have gained more experience and knowledge in the practice of hypnosis, especially in the technique of Past Life Therapy, I have come to realize that it is not enough to help the person to heal their traumas, but it is also necessary to reconcile and balance the feminine and masculine energies. But why is this an important step in the healing process?

- If the energies are not balanced, we will feel incomplete.
- If a man rejects the feminine energy, he will have problems trying to get a partner.
- If a woman rejects the masculine energy, she will have problems trying to get a partner.
- If the feminine energy is damaged, the creative part will be blocked.
- If the masculine energy is damaged, what a woman creates will have no action and projects will not be carried out.
- If the feminine energy is damaged, then we will be disconnected from our essence and our soul.

Let's remember that all this applies to both men and women, because in past lives we have had a different gender. Healing lies in recognizing that both energies live in us, in learning to respect and embrace them, healing them and achieving a perfect balance between them.

Lucy's Disconnection

When I met Lucy, a beautiful 28-year-old, she told me that she was lonely and had never been able to fall in love with anyone. She had had partners before, but had never felt a connection or the love she wanted to feel for them. Lucy attributed this lack of connection to the absence of her father, who was never present in her life, and to certain incidents she had with her stepfather.

Lucy also told me how she had always felt a lack of connection with her mother, feeling that her mother had been with her physically, but not emotionally.

Antonio: As you are breathing in and out, I want you to think about this problem of connection you have with the masculine energy. Let your body feel it. And, as we talk about all this, I want you to feel your body. What does your body experience when it feels this disconnection with the masculine energy?

Lucy: I feel like I want to put my hands up and cross my legs to protect myself from it.

A: Okay, so do that. Feel like you have to protect yourself. If you knew, what do you have to protect yourself from when you cross your arms and your legs?

L: I feel that I have to protect myself because someone wants to rape me [making gestures of discomfort].

A: That's right, experience that even more intensely. What does it feel like when someone wants to rape you?

L: I feel pain in my stomach and everything contracts.

A: Okay, feel that more intensely now. Let your body do whatever it needs to do while I count to three. One, two, three. Where are you while someone is trying to abuse you?

L: I'm in a car with my first boyfriend. We're making out and he's trying to go a little further, but I don't want to.

A: Go on. What else is going on?

L: I end up agreeing.

A: That's it. Feel like you're agreeing, and as you're doing that, what are you feeling?

L: Passive, and I feel almost nothing. I'm not sensitive to touch or anything. I feel numb.

A: What else is going on?

L: He is dominant. He tells me what to do and I end up doing what he wants me to do, but I feel nothing.

Up to this point, Lucy was confirming the way she was interacting with male energy. She was submissive and agreeing to do something she didn't want to do without being able or wanting to perceive more, and feeling completely disconnected.

A: So far, what has been the most difficult moment of this experience?

L: The confusion of seeing how I let this happen.

A: And while you are confused, letting this happen, what are your physical reactions?

L: I can perceive in my brain what I am thinking, but from my neck down I feel nothing.

A: And while you don't feel anything from the neck down, what are your emotional reactions?

L: I resist feeling and try to stay calm and stay in my mental body, trying to make sense of everything.

A: What are your mental reactions?

L: This should not be like this.

A: Now, I want you to remember what this feels like to be in your head refusing to feel, while your head is disconnected from the rest of your body. I'm going to count from three to one, and I want you to go back to another time when you felt the same way. Allow your body to feel whatever it needs to feel and do whatever it needs to do while I count. Three, two, one. You are already there. If you knew, even if you think you are making it, where are you?

L: I am in my mother's womb.

A: That's right, go on.

L: She feels numb.

A: She feels that numbness. Now, ask your mother why she feels that way.

L: She's thinking, 'Why is this happening to me?' [she said, starting to cry].

A: What is she referring to?

L: About being pregnant. She feels sad.

A: See what's going on outside. What are people saying? Where's your father?

L: He's not there, he left her. She's at my grandparents' house with her six siblings. All I see is that she is alone in the house and no one talks to her or cares about her. Everyone is minding their own business, as if it's not a big deal that their first daughter is pregnant.

Here we can begin to notice the instant when Lucy would have begun to feel that disconnection from male energy: her father's abandonment and her mother's lament that she is pregnant, making Lucy feel unwanted.

A: And how do you feel about that?

L: Sad, I feel sad for her.

A: Move forward a little bit more, what else is going on?

L: My grandfather is yelling at her. He's telling her she was stupid, she's not even married, and now she has a baby, so my mom shuts down. She goes numb because it's too much for her.

A: And when your mother disconnects, what happens to you?

L: I think it's not safe to feel. When I ask Lucy to move forward a little bit more, she gets to the time of her birth. Her mother was in the hospital and she was already having some contractions.

A: So far, what has been the most difficult moment of your time in your mother's womb?

L: Not being welcomed.

A: And not being welcomed, what are your physical reactions?

L: I go numb, I disconnect.

A: And as you go to numb, what are your mental reactions?

L: That it is better to stay in my mental body [referring to the fact that it was better not to feel].

A: Now, I want you to see how all this is affecting your life as Lucy. When you say, 'I go numb, I tune out, I don't feel anything, and it's better this way,' what does all this make you do in your life as Lucy?

L: Protect myself.

A: And when you protect yourself, what does that make you do?

L: Try to control the experiences instead of letting them flow naturally.

We continued the therapeutic work by taking Lucy through the birth, as she described to me everything she and her mother were feeling at the time. She also mentioned her desire not to want to be born, to stay in that warmth, in that bubble.

A: And now what is happening?

L: I am outside, but they are taking me away.

A: What happened to your mother?

L: She's in bed breathing heavily.

A: What do you think is happening to her?

L: She has finally processed what just happened [referring to her birth]. She was alone during the birth.

A: Has she been able to hold you in her arms?

L: No.

A: How do you feel?

L: I want to go to her. I want to be with her.

A: You can do that today. You can go to her and feel her energy. Now, ask your mother to give you the energy that she couldn't give you at that moment, your feminine energy. Talk to her and ask her for it.

Lucy asked her mother to please give her the feminine energy that she could not give her at that moment, and she received it by taking it into her chest, into her soul. Then, I helped Lucy identify the emotions she had experienced during her gestation that belonged to her mother: the numbing, the thinking that feeling is not safe and that feeling is dangerous.

That day, during the session, I also asked Lucy to talk to her mother and tell her that she loved her, but that she had to give her back all those emotions that belonged to her. After this exercise, we proceeded to do the energetic cutting of the umbilical cord, stating that once done she would be disconnected from those emotions forever, free to be herself and free of those influences.

So far, we had completed the therapeutic work in this life, but that was not all. We had not yet found the root of those symptoms, which in her life as Lucy she had first experienced in her mother's womb. It was just a matter of asking her spirit to address the event that gave rise to those feelings:

The Roman Soldier and the Young Woman

Antonio: Now I'm going to count from three to one, and I'm going to ask your soul to go to the moment when this all began for her, the event that caused everything in this life. Three, two, one. You are already there. If you knew, even if you think you're imagining it, where are you now? How does this begin for your soul?

Lucy: It is night. I see white temples and I am walking. I am a woman. I'm walking across a path, going to a place and someone dressed as a soldier appears from the left and grabs me by the neck.

A: That's it. Feel all that and go on. [Her face expressed discomfort.] What happens now?

L: He pulls down my dress and bends me over [she said with displeasure and started to cry].

A: That's it, a little more. What else is going on?

L: He's using me. He's using my body for sex [she said, contracting her body and crying].

A: That's it, just a little more. Let your body feel everything it needs to feel. Fast forward to the moment it's over. What's happening to you?

L: He pushes me aside and leaves me there.

A: Fast forward to the next event. What else happens?

L: I lie there until dawn and two women find me. They ask me what happened to me, but I don't say anything. They take me back to my house. I forget what happened and never talk about it again.

A: I want you to move forward to the last moment of that life to see how it ends. Three, two, one. You're already there. What's happening now?

L: I'm in bed, sick. I can't breathe and my lungs feel heavy.

A: Continue.

L: I am an older woman, and I am surrounded by my family.

A: Okay. Up to this point, what has been the most difficult moment in that life?

L: Not talking about this incident with anyone.

A: And at that time, what are your physical reactions?

L: Numbness [she answered, showing that the tendency to numb, to not feel, may have started in that life].

A: And as you feel that numbness, what are your emotional reactions?

L: I feel sad. I don't understand why this had to happen to me.

A: And as you feel sad, what are your mental reactions?

L: Denial.

A: Now, I want you to see how all of this is affecting your life as Lucy, when you go numb, when you feel sad, and when you are in denial. What does this make you do in your life as Lucy?

L: I expect negative experiences.

A: And when you expect negative experiences, what does it prevent you from doing in your life as Lucy?

L: It's as if I have a filter that doesn't allow me to have positive experiences.

Up to this point we had found the event that had originated the pattern of disconnection, numbness, and submission that Lucy was experiencing in her life. Next, I took her back to the rape experience to this time help her desensitize to the traumatic event and to allow her soul to do all that it could not do at the time: defend herself and reclaim the feminine energy that had been stolen from her.

After that, I asked her to go back to the moment of her death and helped her become aware of everything her body was feeling as she was dying. Once out of the body, I began to talk to her spirit.

A: I want you to move the moment you get out of body and look at that life that just ended. What do you think you were supposed to learn in that life?

L: It doesn't make sense, but what comes to my mind is 'make do with certain things'.

A: You don't have to make sense of anything. Now, I want you to see how that relates to Lucy's life. What is it that you have to get right in Lucy's life?

L: That certain things are not mine [she replied, referring to the programming she carried in her mind from her time in her mother's womb].

A: So, you are keeping everything in your head. Even when this older woman passed away, you kept everything in your head. You chose to disconnect; you chose not to think and to go numb. But that event belongs to that body, to that life, and it doesn't make sense that in Lucy's body you have to keep disconnecting and numbing yourself every time she is in this situation with someone that she loves, that she likes. Does that make sense?

L: No.

A: Give yourself permission to feel with your whole body, with your heart, with your sexual organs. It's not about keeping everything in the mind. The mind dies with the body. It's time for you to start feeling with your soul.

After a few more minutes, I started to bring Lucy out of the hypnotic trance. She had cried a lot and her makeup was smeared. The session had been very intense and emotional for her, but she was able to understand the origin of her patterns that were present in her current life. She was able to end her soul entrapment and regain her feminine energy, both in the past life in which she had been raped, and in her current life in Lucy's body.

A few days later I decided to call her to ask her how she had been doing after the session. She told me that thanks to the session, she had been able to realize the connection issues she had faced throughout her life and that she had been repeating her mother's pattern with men. She also told me that she now felt vulnerable, revealing that she no longer felt disconnected from her emotions.

The Boy on the Train

Some pages ago I commented that it is not only the feminine energy that can be damaged, but also the masculine one. The case of Joost, a charismatic young man who came to my office, is a clear example of this. When he was a child, his relationship with his father was abruptly severed after his mother decided to separate. Joost never received an explanation, nor the real reason why she decided to leave home.

During the initial interview he also mentioned that he did not have many memories of his childhood, something that to me could mean that his conscious mind had blocked out traumatic memories from that time.

Antonio: I want you to look for a sad memory, some event that affected you or made you feel bad. I'll count from three to one, and you'll be there. Three, two, one. You're already there.

Joost: The first thing that comes to mind is that I'm on a train.

A: Alright, go ahead. What's going on?

J: I'm with my mother and my two brothers. We've left.

A: Go on. What else is going on?

J: I'm surprised.

A: What did your mother tell you? Why are you on that train?

J: Because it's not safe to stay. My mother says we are going to a safe place now.

A: And how do you feel about that?

J: Bad because I didn't get to say goodbye to my friends at school.

A: How does that make you feel?

J: I feel sad.

A: Feel all that more intensely, as that train takes you away from your home, your friends, and your father. What else happens on that train?

J: I'm confused and crying.

A: Then let that child cry because he has every right to cry. He's confused and he's going somewhere else, somewhere safe. What did your mother tell you? Why weren't you sure?

J: My father tried to strangle my mother.

At this point, making use of the role change technique, I decided to ask him to let me talk to his mother.

A: Let me talk to your mother. Three, two, one. Switch. Mary Ann, thank you for the communication. I see you're on a train going away with your children. What's going on? Why are you leaving with your children?

Mary Ann: It's not safe to stay [she replied in a firm voice] not for me and not for my children.

A: Have you explained this to Joost?

M: I have tried, but he is still very young.

A: He's so confused, leaving home, moving away from his friends. He doesn't understand what's going on.

What have you told him so far? Have you told him what your husband tried to do to you?

M: No.

Mary Ann was reluctant to tell Joost why she had decided to leave home with them. Her husband, Joost's father, had tried to strangle her in one of his constant episodes of violence. She went on to tell me that he was too young, that he wouldn't understand, and that she would tell him years later when he was older. After a few more minutes of conversation, Mary Ann agreed to tell him what happened, but, as we will see later, she did not tell him everything.

A: He's listening. Talk to him.

M: I love you. This is for your own safety and mine too [she said getting emotional] What if he hurts you or hurts your brothers? What if he killed me next time?

A: Mary Ann, tell him what your husband did to you.

M: He becomes someone else. He gets upset and very violent. He tried to strangle me.

A: Joost, did you listen to your mother, do you understand what she is saying?

J: Yes [he answered with a sad expression].

A: Do you understand that they are leaving for your own safety? What would you do to protect your mother from your father?

J: I don't know.

A: You are very young. The only thing you can do to protect her is to go with her, to be with her. She needs you, doesn't she?

J: Yes.

A: Now you understand why they are leaving and you don't have to feel confused anymore. You are leaving so that your mother and you are safe. So far, what has been the most difficult moment of this experience with your mother and siblings on the train?

J: Not knowing what was going on.

A: And while that's happening, what are your physical reactions?

J: I feel it in my throat, both in that memory and as I sit here.

A: What are your emotional reactions?

J: I feel difficulty expressing myself.

A: What are your mental reactions as you have difficulty expressing yourself?

J: I feel everything here in my throat.

A: Now feel your throat. What is happening to your throat? What kind of feeling is this in your throat?

J: It feels like something is strangling me.

A: Feel that more intensely. I'm going to count from three to one, and I want you to go to the first moment you felt that way. Three, two, one. You're already there. If you knew, even if you think you're imagining it, where are you while you feel like you're being strangled?

J: I feel like I'm being squeezed [he said, gesturing uncomfortably].

A: If you knew, where are you while you're being squeezed? That's right, feel all that.

At that moment, Joost began to throw his head back as if someone was choking him. His neck showed a red spot and I could see on his face how uncomfortable he felt.

J: I feel like I'm too young.

A: Are you a man or a woman? [I asked, trying to figure out if it was an event from this life or a previous one].

J: I am a man.

A: And what do they call you there?

J: Joost.

A: Alright, Joost. If you knew, where are you?

J: It's my father!

A: Go on. What's going on?

J: It's uncomfortable [with great difficulty breathing]. He's trying to strangle me.

A: If you knew, why is he trying to strangle you?

J: He's not himself.

A: What is your body feeling?

J: A lot of pressure on my neck. It's making it hard for me to talk.

A: Approximately how old are you there?

J: Two years [tears running down his face].

A: So far, Joost, what has been the most difficult moment of that experience with your father?

J: Not having control.

A: And while you're not in control, what are your physical reactions?

J: I panic.

A: And while you are panicking, what are your emotional reactions?

J: I think I shut down.

A: And when you're shutting down, what are your mental reactions?

J: I go inside myself.

A: Now, I want you to see how all of this is affecting your life as a Joost, when you panic, you shut down and go inside yourself. What does all of that do to you in your life as a Joost?

J: It makes me not express myself enough.

A: What does that stop you from doing?

J: Speaking my truth.

In this session we had encountered a memory that had been repressed, that had been erased from Joost's conscious mind, one that he obviously did not remember. In that experience his father was out of his mind. He used to drink alcohol, and when that happened, he was transformed.

When he learned what his father had tried to do to him, he could understand what his mother meant when she said it was not safe to stay at home. At last he understood what had happened and the reason they were on that train running away from his father.

After helping him complete what was pending for his soul, and having done the therapeutic work, I proceeded to bring him out of the hypnotic trance. Once the session was over I could tell that he looked surprised, as if trying to make sense of what he had just experienced. Joost burst into tears as he understood, I guess, what his mother had done to protect them. She hadn't actually run away just for her safety, but also to protect him and his siblings. Joost was now going to be able to express himself better and break the pattern of feeling good about being alone and being introverted.

RAPE AND MOLESTATION

In the chapter The Purpose of the Soul I briefly explained how the spirit world works and how it is that the spirit chooses the lessons and situations it will have to face once reincarnated. However, the events of sexual abuse have always made me doubt the validity of this spiritual principle. It is clear to me that it matters little what I, from my vision inside a human body, may believe in this regard, but the truth is that this is so. As reported by several of my clients in hypnotic trance, their spirits chose to experience this type of circumstances because they needed to learn something from them or simply because it was their turn to experience them as a consequence of karma, that is, that now it was their turn to go through what they had made others go through in a past life.

To help the victim of these events to let go of this experience, many therapists choose to use de-victimization. This concept, which is still a topic of discussion among the therapeutic community, consists of guiding the victim to let go of that role so that he or she can regain control of his or her life. The reason several of us use this technique is because if the spirit chose that lesson for itself or it is the result of its past actions (karma), then it cannot be considered a victim of the situation. I am aware that certain trends in clinical hypnosis are totally against this method and that while they work on desensitizing the trauma, they also focus on providing the necessary support to the one they consider the victim.

In the following pages I will use the word *victim*, but only with the intention of identifying the role that the affected person is playing in that experience. We all play three roles in our lives: victim, perpetrator, and observer.

As I mentioned in the previous chapter, I have devoted an entire chapter to the events of rape and molestation, as these types of traumatic events can be experienced during childhood, youth, and adulthood, as well as in past lives. Remember that for the soul, time does not exist. Regardless of when and where it has had that experience, the symptom of it will manifest in the present at the physical, emotional, mental, and energetic levels. Rape and molestation are among the most traumatic memories a person can visit during a hypnotic trance state. I can say this without fear of contradiction. Reliving these traumas is not only difficult for those who came to a session in search of help, but also for all of us who practice this type of hypnosis, in which the aim is for the soul to process the painful events by reliving them in order to desensitize the trauma.

A person in a trance state who returns to their rape, for example, will relive in front of us (the therapists) the moment in which they were assaulted, experiencing everything they experienced in that past event as if it were happening right now. There have been several times that I have seen the person move violently, cry with helplessness, scream and struggle as if they were being assaulted in front of us. Sometimes the person will go to these memories spontaneously, but sometimes the therapist will guide the person to the memories in order to work on them. Whatever the case may be, this is one of the most complicated tasks a therapist can face, especially if they themselves were victims of this type of situation.

The biggest mistake made by spiritual hypnosis therapists is to think that, in order to help our clients or patients, it is only necessary to visit past lives, guide the person to establish communication with their Higher Self—the part of us that is connected to the spirit world and has a better understanding—and visit sad memories of the current life, while avoiding contact with strong emotions or re-experiencing their former pain. In other words, we could say that some hypnotherapists accompany their patients during the session as if they were watching the movie of their life without allowing them to make contact with the intense feelings and physical sensations that ultimately caused the trauma.

Some hypnosis practitioners who are new to this journey will even say that they prefer not to have their clients visit traumatic events altogether in order to avoid retraumatizing the person and to prevent the trauma from becoming any worse. However, I have found that a good number of therapists use this as an excuse not to relive these experiences, not only because it might be uncomfortable for their patient, but also because it is uncomfortable for them.

We must understand that in order to desensitize any traumatic event, the person must relive it again to a certain extent in the company of their therapist. I use this method in my sessions with excellent results, but I did not invent it myself. Michael Newton, in his book *Life Between Lives*, describes it as part of the work process. In addition, during my training in Past Life Therapy with José Luis Cabouli, he emphasized that trauma cannot be made worse than it already is and that for him retraumatization does not exist.

If we remember the concepts we have previously explored, the event of rape or inappropriate touching can be totally or partially blocked by the conscious mind of the individual. The conscious mind tends to repress and remove traumatic experiences that can overload us and sends them to the subconscious. Consequently, we do not consciously remember them; rather the symptoms suddenly appear when we go through similar situations.

More than once I have had clients mention having vague memories or spontaneous images of something that supposedly happened to them in childhood, but they did not know what it was despite their suspicions. Even though they did not remember the events, they had all the symptoms of a victim of sexual abuse. Still these people did not understand why they were experiencing all kinds of symptoms while having sexual intercourse. It was during the hypnotic state, by going back to the traumatic event and experiencing it again, that they not only remembered what had happened, but were also able to heal.

The effects of rape can be devastating. They affect the victim not only on a physical, mental, and emotional level, but also on an energetic and soul level. Although when we think of rape victims, we commonly think first of a woman, in reality a man can also suffer the same type of attack and on an emotional, mental, spiritual, and soul level have the same consequences.

In the case of a rape during childhood, I have observed that the effects are usually even more serious than if it happened at an adult age because the kid's childhood is taken away from them leaving a mark that will last their entire life. These cases are more complicated when the rapist is part of the victim's family circle, whether it is the father, stepfather, brother, grandfather, uncle or even close family friends. To learn how a child tries to understand and process what is being done to them, I will mention some phrases pronounced by clients in a hypnotic state who returned to a childhood rape or inappropriate touching event:

- "My grandfather has laid down on my bed, and while he is hugging me, I feel like he has peed himself."
- "My uncle is asking me to touch his parts."
- "My father is hugging me, and I feel like he is poking me with something."
- "I feel like a rag doll as I am being turned around and touched."

When the rapist belongs to the family circle, the abused child cannot understand what is happening and why a loved one is doing this to them. Many times, in order not to be discovered, the rapist will tell the little one phrases like:

- "This is a secret between you and me."
- "This is how you show affection."
- "If you are good to me, I will give you a prize."
- "If you tell your parents, they won't believe you."
- "I'm doing this with you because you are special."

These phrases will not only generate great confusion in them in the moment, but in a way they will program their behavior for when they grow up and try to establish a relationship with their partner.

Another sad case that occurs within sexual abuse is when the child speaks up, but the parents completely discredit the account of the sexual assault, either out of blind love for the abuser or out of fear. In these cases, the young victim is not only damaged by the rape and the symptoms that result, but also by a feeling of abandonment by the parents, affecting their self-esteem and credibility.

Physical Symptoms

For female rape victims, they may experience some of the following symptoms:

- Vaginal or anal bleeding
- Hypoactive sexual desire disorder or lack of interest in sexual activity
- Vaginal swelling
- Dyspareunia, which is a painful sensation when attempting intercourse or other penetrative sexual activities
- Vaginismus, which is the involuntary contraction of the muscles around the opening of the vagina
- Urinary tract infection

Psychological and Emotional Symptoms

- Feelings of fear
- Nervousness
- Panic attacks
- Flashbacks
- Nightmares
- Feelings of guilt

Symptoms at the Energetic and Soul Level

These are some of the consequences of violation at this level, regardless of whether it has taken place in childhood, adolescence, adulthood, or during a past life:

- The theft of energy
- The wounding of the feminine energy
- Fragmentation of the soul

In the previous chapter we talked about the masculine and feminine energies and how their imbalance produces different symptoms in a human being. Rape, in this case, directly affects the feminine and creative energy, also causing soul entrapment in such an event. Something else that can happen during this type of event, regardless of the age of the victim, is the fragmentation of the soul or detachment of the part of the soul that could not bear the emotional and physical pain of that event.

On several occasions, during the hypnosis sessions I facilitate, I have come across people who were abused multiple times during childhood and as a result their soul had repeatedly fragmented. When reliving these events, people in hypnotic trance described it using phrases such as:

- "I'm out of there."
- "I'm out of my body."
- "I'm seeing everything from above."
- "I fall asleep and wake up when it's all over."
- "Suddenly everything goes dark."

This happened to them so many times that even the child learned that in order to avoid pain and facing this traumatic event, he or she had to disconnect and get out of his or her body. This behavior continued into their adult life, where every time they had to face a difficult event in their life, they would fragment.

During the interview prior to the hypnosis session and sharing their symptoms with me, many clients have unknowingly given me clues that they have suffered one or more fragmentations. They describe their symptoms this way:

- "I don't feel in my body."
- "I can't feel emotions."
- "I can think love, but I can't feel it."

- "I only realize I have cut myself when I see myself bleeding, but I don't feel the cut."
- "When I am intimate with my partner, I don't get to feel anything."

All of this indicated a clear disconnection of their soul from the physical body, the result of soul fragmentation and having done it for so long that they now did it almost automatically.

These same people also had difficulty connecting on an emotional level with family, friends, and partners. In the case of couples, the greatest frustration was felt during sexual relations because they could not establish the desired connection with the loved one or simply felt that they could not give them the pleasure they wanted to because they did not feel present in those moments of intimacy. Many times, I heard from my clients that they could not reach orgasm. On more than one occasion, they even expressed their frustration for never having been able to experience one, causing great frustration in their partners.

Helping to Complete the Experience

When a person wants a hypnosis session because they present symptoms that have no logic or scientific explanation, this makes me suspect that they come from a traumatic experience. From the approach of spirituality, when we speak of traumatic experience, we are not only referring to events in this life, but also to those we face in other bodies and other lives.

Trauma is understood as an event that the soul could not complete on a physical, emotional, or mental level. We have also said that when this event is not processed correctly, our soul remains trapped in that experience, making us feel or react as if all of it was still happening. Let's also remember that, in order to desensitize a trauma, a person has to experience it again by the therapist, that is they should be helped to relive the rape by asking their body to feel everything it has to feel in order to complete that experience. This would be, so to speak, the most difficult part of the therapeutic work.

Then, if we think about what may have been left pending or what the soul lacked to complete during that experience, the answers could be varied, but this is what I have found in the sessions:

- Being able to defend themselves
- Getting the rapist off themselves
- Being able to tell others what happened to them
- Not being ignored by sharing what happened
- To be heard
- Finding justice

These pending issues may be different, and we therapists should not assume what they are. This information should come from the victim themself after having relived the traumatic event in a hypnotic state, asking the following question: "What has been the most difficult moment of this experience up to this point?"

We then help the person understand the physical, emotional, and mental reactions during that moment and how they are affecting them in their current life: what it makes them do and what it prevents them from doing.

In this way we are guiding the soul to understand the symptoms or patterns of behavior that this event has generated in it, but to complete the therapeutic work, we will ask the soul to:

1. Go back once again to the beginning of the experience, but this time do whatever they have to do to get the abuser off of them. This is where we give the person the opportunity to stand up for themselves, to do everything now that they could not do then. We are also giving them the voice and authority that the victim did not have at the time, even more so if the rape occurred during her childhood.

2. Let them speak to the perpetrator and demand that they give them back the energy they stole from them, making them take it and bring it into their soul again.

3. Have them tell us where their soul is while all of this is going on. This will help us determine if there was a fragmentation of the soul as a result of the rape.

4. If the answer is similar to the expressions I shared in the energetic and soul symptoms section, being able to determine that there

was a fragmentation, we will ask the patient to talk to the part of the soul that was fragmented, ask it to come back, and assure it that it will be protected, that no one will do that to it again, and that they need to be together to feel whole and complete with all their energy.

The Slave on the Boat

During one of the workshops I taught on entrapment and recovery of the soul, when choosing the third and final volunteer for the demonstration sessions, Iris' name came up.

After a short interview I asked her, "What does your soul need today?" She replied that her body was not feeling well and that she felt a pain in her lower abdomen that did not allow her to enjoy sex with her partner. She told me that when it was time to have sex and feel her partner, her body would tense up in such a way that it caused her unbearable pain.

The doctors she had seen could not find a logical reason for what she was experiencing. Physically she was fine, but she had never been able to experience the typical passion and excitement in her sexual relations.

Over the years, Iris realized that she had been looking for love through sex, until she understood that if a man wanted to have sex, it was not because he necessarily felt love for her. She became emotional as she told me that she had a partner but could not give him sexually what she wanted.

Antonio: Take a deep breath and close your eyes. Let the mattress absorb your body without any resistance. Let's allow your soul to work today, and I will be here to accompany it as far as it wants to go. And you will follow it as far as it wants to go.

Now, I want you to go back to one of those intimate moments with this person you love. And, while this is taking place, tell me what you are feeling: your emotions and what your body is experiencing.

Iris: My uterus hurts.

A: Okay. Feel that more intensely, feel that pain. And that pain in the uterus, what does it feel like is happening to it? If you knew, what kind of pain is it?

I: The pain is warm.

A: That's right, you feel that. And this warm pain is similar to what, what is happening to your uterus? Maybe it feels like a pressure or stabbing pain.

I: It feels more like a stabbing.

A: Very good! Now make it more intense. If you knew, even if you think you're imagining it, as you feel that warm, stabbing pain in your uterus, where are you? Follow that symptom and let it take you back to another time where you experienced the same thing, as I count from three to one. Three, two, one. Where are you now?

I: I feel like I am on a boat. I am a slave on the boat.

A: Continue.

I: I am a slave for pleasure [moaning in annoyance].

A: What's happening?

I: Oh my God! [crying in pain and touching her belly] Stop, please! Please, I can't take it anymore!

A: Continue. What's happening?

I: I'm being raped! I feel like a toilet.

A: That's it, go on a little more.

I: It's so painful, please stop! I can only feel my pain. My heart is not well either. I'm not an animal! I'm a woman!

I: Continue. What else is happening?

I: They are choking me [putting her hands to her neck and showing difficulty breathing, while continuing to cry]. I can't talk, I can't say anything.

A few seconds later, I could see how Iris' face and body relaxed and began to breathe normally again. Apparently, that rape had ended with the death of that body.

A: So far, what has been the most difficult moment of this experience?

I: When they don't respect me.

A: And while you are not respected, what are your physical reactions?

I: I'm kind of frozen.

A: And while you are frozen there, what are your emotional reactions?

I: It's so sad!

A: And while you're feeling kind of frozen and sad, what are your mental reactions?

I: Why are they doing this to me? Why?

A: Now I want you to see how this is affecting your life as Iris. When you freeze, you feel sad, and you wonder why they are doing this to you, what is this doing to you in your life as Iris?

I: I freeze and I don't do anything. I don't move forward. I just stand here, and I don't fight for myself.

A: And all this, what does it stop you from doing?

I: Fight for my rights, fight for my voice.

A: Okay, now I'm going to count from three to one, and I want you to go to the moment when this experience starts, to the moment when all this starts in that life. Let your body feel everything it needs to feel. Three, two, one. You are already there. How does this experience begin?

I: I am in my land, in the jungle. We are a small tribe. We live in peace and we are peaceful, but we have been attacked.

A: Look who is attacking them.

I: Slave traders. They kill my family, my father, my mother, and my sister [breaking down in tears]. They are gone! They have chained me and others, and we will be taken away from here. I fight! And because I fight like a tigress, they rape me. I must not fight, but I have to fight because I am a human being.

As she recounted how she struggled to defend herself, the men began to rape her. The young woman had gone back to the moment when she was being raped on the boat, the one that would end her life.

It does not matter how much experience one may have as a hypnotist or hypnotherapist. Accompanying a person in trance who suffers a rape is always a difficult and uncomfortable experience to observe, even though we know that in order to eliminate a trauma or the entrapment of the soul, it is necessary to relive the event.

Iris began to move as if someone was holding her and her neck began to show red marks. She opened her mouth as if she was trying to gasp for air so she could breathe, while crying and feeling totally helpless.

I: They have started to rape me [breathing quickly]. I can't take it anymore! This is too much.

A: Continue. What else is happening?

I: I can't move because they are holding me to the ground. They are choking me.

A: I'm going to count from three to one and you're going to let yourself feel everything more intensely. Three, two, one. What is your uterus feeling while you are being raped?

I: I feel pain [crying uncontrollably]. I am disgusted and I don't want to have this inside me. This is disgusting. Oh, my God. [These last words would have been part of the command that her soul would carry into the next life, into the life of Iris: "I don't want this inside me," referring to her rapist's penis.] They are choking me and I can't breathe [showing red marks on her neck and with clear difficulty in breathing and speaking]. I can't scream because of all this pain. I can't breathe anymore; I'm going to die!

A: What are you thinking while they are doing that to you?

I: I don't deserve this! I don't deserve this!

A: Now move to the moment they finish.

As soon as I gave her that instruction, she began to gasp as she said that she couldn't breathe and that her lungs couldn't take it anymore. After that, her body relaxed completely, and she began to breathe normally. The young woman had already passed away.

A: Now I want you to talk to those who did that to you and ask them to give you back your energy right now.

I: Give me back my female energy now! It belongs to me, it's mine!

A: When you are ready, take your energy and take it to your soul again, understanding that with the death of that body, that is over and none of it belongs to you anymore.

The session continued for a few more minutes as we completed the final steps of Past Life Therapy for cases of rape.

Iris' soul had been trapped in that life because her body had not been able to process the death physically, emotionally, and mentally. That is why during the time I accompanied her in that past life, I asked her all kinds of questions to help her become aware of everything that had been left incomplete.

Her soul, trapped in that experience, made her relive everything she felt in that life when she was raped during sexual relations with her partner. In addition, there was the disposition she pronounced before she died: "I don't want this inside me." For this reason, her body reacted that way. For Iris' soul, she was still being raped.

The Sacrificial Young Woman

During a demonstration session in one of the workshops I taught called Healing the Wounded Feminine Energy, Megan volunteered. From the beginning I could see her nervousness in answering the questions I asked her to understand what it was she wanted to heal. Megan recognized a behavioral pattern in herself, in which she could not get out of abusive relationships. In fact she said that she was in an abusive relationship at the time. One of the things that made her react was when she was blamed for everything that happened in the relationship.

I decided to include this session in this chapter on rape because that is part of what was affecting her. But in this case, you can see how a little bit of everything takes place, including timeless phrases, the wounded feminine energy, going from being a victim to being a perpetrator in a way in her quest for revenge and entrapment in the womb.

Antonio: What do you feel when they say it's all your fault? What do you feel in your body?

Megan: A lot of pain and fear.

A: Okay, feel that pain more intensely.

M: And fear.

A: Where do you feel that pain in your body?

M: In my abdomen and in my sexual organs.

A: And this pain that you feel, what does it feel like? What is happening to your body?

M: Like I'm being cut open.

A: It feels like you are being cut open. Experience this pain. And if you knew, even if you think you are making it up, where are you when you feel this pain as you are being cut open?

M: On some kind of big rock. It's like a ritual, but I don't understand.

A: You don't have to understand, just describe to me what is happening.

M: I'm being sacrificed.

A: Go on a little bit more. Feel everything.

M: They are dancing around me, invoking something. I think they are afraid of me too.

A: What else is happening?

M: I know they are going to kill me. I have cuts all over my body, and I'm bleeding [with a painful expression].

A: Feel all that and move forward a little more.

M: They are going to cut me open and take out my organs, God knows for what purpose. But that is their intention.

A: Continue a little more.

M: They're cutting me open now [with tears in her eyes]. I'm screaming that I haven't done anything, that I don't deserve this, and they tell me to shut up. Some of them laugh.

A: What else is going on? Continue.

M: I just feel dizzy. I think I've lost a lot of blood and I'm going to go.

A: Then let that body die. Now I'm going to count from three to one, and when I get to one, I want you to go to the beginning of this experience, to the beginning of that life to know what happened. Let your body feel whatever it has to feel now. Three, two one. You are already there. If you knew, how does this all start?

M: I live in a village. It's very primitive, and I'm a little different from others. My way of thinking is different. I'm not as scared as they are, and I have different theories than they have about life and about where we come from. Some are scared, and some think I'm crazy.

A: How old are you there?

M: About 15 years. I'm young, and I'm a woman.

A: What are you wearing?

M: Like a dress, but it's kind of dirty. I'm poor.

A: Continue. What else happens?

M: Eventually they get tired of me. They want to shut me up; they don't want to hear me anymore. I'm a nuisance to them.

A: Move to the moment something happens. Three, two, one. You're already there.

M: They're taking my mother away, and I never see her again. I think they're going to kill her.

A: And why do you think they took your mother away?

M: My mother is also different. She knows about plants. She makes medicine with them, and she has been blamed for something, but it's not her fault. I feel so sad and so lonely because she was the only person who understood me.

A: That's right, feel all of that. Move forward to the moment when something happens to you. Three, two, one. You're already there.

M: They want to kill me just like they did her.

A: Move forward to the moment when they come for you. Where are you now?

M: I'm in my house. It's a small shack and there are several people outside asking me to come out or they're going to burn the house down.

A: That's right, go on.

M: I don't know what to do. I don't like either option, but I hope I can convince them, so I go outside. I ask them why they are coming for me. They think I'm a witch.

A: What happens next?

M: They rip off my dress [she replied with annoyance], and I feel so embarrassed. I want to cover myself and they laugh. They are hitting me. I hate them all! I want them to suffer as I am suffering and as my mother suffered."

A: Go on. What else is going on?

M: I am planning my revenge in case I manage to escape. I will set fire to the whole village.

Up to this point, the young woman accused of being a witch, faced with a moment of despair and suffering, uttered a couple of timeless phrases: "I hate you all," and "I want you to suffer." Both would bring consequences for her in a future life. The second phrase we can describe as a kind of curse that also brings effects to the soul, as I explained in the chapter Timeless Phrases.

A: Once they catch you and take your clothes off, what happens?

M: They take me to a cell and I am raped many times. I feel a lot of pain and my legs hurt a lot.

A: Why do your legs hurt?

M: Because I have been chained for many days.

A: Up to this point, what has been the most difficult moment of this experience of this life?

M: Not understanding. I feel that it is so unfair and that I am not crazy. They are crazy. They are stupid; how come they can't see what I see?

A: And while you don't have this understanding, what are your physical reactions?

M: Rage. I have so much anger.

A: And when you feel that rage, what are your emotional reactions?

M: I am shattered, and I cry a lot. I want to leave. I just wish for my death. I don't see any point in staying.

A: And what are your mental reactions?

M: There is no mental stability anymore. I start to doubt myself too.

A: Now I want you to see how all this is affecting your life as Megan. All these feelings of anger, being destroyed, crying a lot, and having lost your mental stability, what does it make you do in your life as Megan?

M: Run away from people, cut them off. Have very difficult relationships with men.

A: What does this stop you from doing?

M: Creating meaningful and healthy relationships, really connecting, letting people in, showing who I really am.

Up to this point Megan had been able to find the origin of the behavior pattern that was preventing her from getting out of abusive relationships, also the origin of her disproportionate reaction when she was told she was wrong, that it was all her fault, or that it was all a product of her perception.

In the following minutes I helped her complete that experience, to do all that had been pending for her soul while I took her back to the scene of death where she died from the cuts that were made. Once out of the body, I continued to work with her:

A: Now I want you to see something else. The phrase "I hate them all" that you said, what does it make you do in your life as Megan?

M: I want revenge.

A: When you wish that on someone, that same thing comes back to you multiplied times three.

M: It's not conscious, and I can't help it. It comes back to me all the time.

A: Curses always come back, as you are experiencing in Megan's life. By saying you want them to feel what you felt, you make that energy projected to them come back to you. To fix it, I want you to break that thing you said, but for that you need to forgive.

M: Forgiveness is very difficult. What is forgiveness? Finally, how can you forgive this?

A: Forgiveness does not mean to forget, nor does it mean to be friends with your perpetrator or to stop seeking justice. Forgiveness is to stop taking a poison waiting for others to die, when in reality you are killing yourself. Should we stop taking that poison today?

M: I forgive them.

A: Now look for the energy of that curse. Where in your body have you been storing it?

M: In my stomach.

So Megan proceeded to forgive, retracting what she had said, and then proceeded to remove the energy she had been storing in her stomach. Now we had to find out if her soul needed to heal anything else.

One of the things she had mentioned during our short pre-session interview was the disconnection she felt with her parents.

A: Now I want you to go to another time where there is something your soul needs to heal. Three, two, one. You are already there.

M: I think I'm in my mother's womb.

A: Okay, then experience this dark, wet environment. Feel your body float.

M: I'm going to die [interrupting me].

A: What makes you think you are going to die?

M: My mother has been praying to God for me to die [crying]. She is very young and has just married my father and wants more time and is asking God to take me. She is not ready.

A: How do you feel about that?

M: I feel very sorry for her. I don't want to bother her. I don't want to make anyone uncomfortable.

A: What is she feeling right now?

M: She is not well. She feels very sick and vomits all the time. She hasn't been able to eat for several days.

A: How do you feel while that is going on?

M: I feel so sorry for her. I want to hug her and comfort her. I'm sorry for causing so much damage. I didn't mean to.

A: Listen to what's going on outside, with your father, with your grandparents. What's going on?

M: They are not happy. My father is not happy. They are students, and my father will have to leave university to get a job, and he is very stressed. They are arguing a lot. He yells at my mother.

A: What is he saying?

M: That it's her fault for getting pregnant. He's saying something really nasty to her.

A: What is he saying to her?

M: He doesn't think I'm his daughter. He thinks my mother cheated on him.

A: And what are you feeling while he's saying all this?

M: I want to protect her. I want to come out, look him in the eye, and tell him he is so wrong.

A: So, what has been the most difficult moment during your time in your mother's womb?

M: The moment when she prayed to God that I would die. The placenta was detaching, I'm not sure. It felt like it was starting to go down.

A: And at that moment, what are your physical reactions?

M: I'm very scared. I curl up into a little ball and try to protect myself.

A: And what are your emotional reactions?

M: I feel helpless.

A: And what are your mental reactions?

M: I think I deserve to leave because I have caused so much damage. I'm bracing myself for impact, I'm bracing myself to fall.

A: Now I want you to see how all this is affecting your life as Megan, when you say that you are scared, that you are cowering like a little ball to protect yourself, that you feel helpless, and you deserve to leave because of all the damage you have caused. What does all this make you do in your life as Megan?

M: Trying to please them. Everything revolves around my parents, even when I know they are not right and that I deserve to live my life the way I want to. I feel so guilty.

A: And when that happens, what does it stop you from doing?

M: Being happy and enjoying my life. I don't seek relationships with other people.

A: And when you say, "I deserve to leave for all the damage I have caused," what does that make you do?

M: Actually, wanting to leave. I've thought about that many times.

Through her time in her mother's womb, we were able to find valuable information about her pattern of behavior, not only with her parents, but also with her partners, not being able to get out of abusive relationships and also feeling disconnected from everything.

After this I guided her through her birth, helping her to understand that all those emotions that she had made her own, in reality, belonged to her mother. She was not to blame for anything. I then proceeded to disconnect those emotions to complete the therapeutic work.

THE ROLES WE PLAY IN OUR LIVES

So far, we have seen how the soul brings different symptoms that may have been generated as a consequence of its entrapment in other experiences. We have also seen the types of death, timeless phrases, wounded male and female energies, and the events of rape and molestation, to name a few. All of these conditions can affect us here and now regardless of when the original event took place. Now I consider it essential to briefly mention another of the concepts I learned from my great teacher, José Luis Cabouli, which helped me to refine and redefine my approach to therapies with my clients.

This concept consists of the roles that we play in our past lives and in the current one, that in one way or another have affected us in a past life and without even knowing it the current one and even a future one. These roles are basically three: victim, perpetrator, and observer. Each of them will impact us in a different way, but it could be said that the result will be the same: a symptom, a behavior pattern that in many cases can lead us to self-sabotage in our lives.

Let's look at what each of these roles means and how they can impact us:

The Victim

The Real Academia de la Lengua Española dictionary provides the following definitions:

- Person or animal sacrificed or destined for sacrifice
- Person who exposes or offers themselves to serious risk as a gift to another
- Person who suffers harm due to the fault of another or due to a fortuitous cause
- A person who dies through the fault of another or by fortuitous accident
- Person who suffers the harmful consequences of a crime

For the purposes of the subject we are dealing with in this book, the definition that best fits would be the third one. I am referring to all those who consider themselves harmed by a third party or by fortuitous cause, although I know that coincidences do not really exist.

The role of victim does not allow us to take ownership of our own actions, nor to take responsibility for the part that corresponds to us. When you feel like a victim, you simply blame someone else for everything that happens to you, be it someone else, fate, bad luck or even God himself, if you think that what you are experiencing is a punishment.

While it is true that this role is the most harmful to our spiritual evolution, it is actually the most comfortable to adopt because we simply allow ourselves to be a kind of leaf in the wind at the mercy of wherever it takes us. In the same way, people who find themselves playing the role of victim feel that they have no free will, that they have no escape, and that they are trapped in the event that is happening to them or with the person who is victimizing them.

For this reason, the most difficult thing to achieve in a spiritual hypnosis session is to get the person out of the victim mentality, which is only delaying their spiritual evolution and the lessons they came to learn in this incarnation. The problem can be even more serious when this role is carried over from other lives, generating a pattern of self-sabotage.

Something relevant to mention is that in reality every victim has been a perpetrator before. In a hypnosis session, in order to understand when the role of victim was generated in our client, we must ask them to go to the event that originated what they are experiencing. Thus, we will be surprised to find that they were the perpetrator in that event.

I remember one of the Introspective Hypnosis courses I taught in 2019. On the last day of the training I asked for a volunteer for a demonstration session. A middle-aged woman volunteered, and so it was that I began with the process of hypnotic induction, then proceeded to visit sad or traumatic memories. The first memory she came to was one in which she was a child and tearfully recounted how a family member had come into her room during the night and started touching her private parts. In the second memory she visited she had grown up a bit, but the situation was basically the same. On that occasion it had been a family friend who had gone into her room to touch her. In the third memory she was already a teenager, but the situation repeated itself with someone around her. It was at this point that she screamed, "Not again! Why me?!"

At that point I told her we would find out why. I counted from three to one and asked her to address the event that had originated this for her soul. Suddenly, she told me that she was a soldier during wartime and described how he would break into houses and rape women because he had been alone for some time and because he needed to. It was interesting to observe how the woman's cry in the current life became a face that showed pleasure as he raped defenseless women. In that life he had been a perpetrator. Now, in the current life, it was her turn to experience what the soldier made those women experience.

In sessions with other clients, I was able to observe how in a past life they had done things they regretted before, during, or after the death of that body. It was not until they became aware of what they had done and what they had caused, that they pronounced a timeless phrase such as:

- "I do not deserve to be forgiven."
- "I don't deserve to be happy."
- "No matter how many lives I live, I will not be able to pay off this debt."

These phrases were what turned them from perpetrators to victims, self-sabotaging themselves in their current life because on a subconscious and spiritual level, they felt they did not deserve to be happy or forgiven. Every time they were on the verge of happiness, they did something without realizing that it would end it.

What happens, then, when we play the role of victim? From my point of view, we are giving our energy to the one we consider our perpetrator. When we give our energy, we are giving them control, and as a result part of our energy can get trapped in that event. We have already seen how the soul does not understand time, and no matter how much time has passed since that event, we will experience the symptoms (consequences) of that event as if it were happening right now because to our soul it is.

The Perpetrator

The perpetrator is the one who inflicts harm on someone at a given moment, causing them to become a victim. So starting from this definition and observing this role from the perception of an incarnated spirit, that is from our perception while we are incarnated in a human body, we could consider the perpetrator as someone who is bad and deserves punishment for the harm and suffering they caused.

But in reality, to understand this role in depth we would have to shed our physical body and look at it from the point of view of spirituality. On several occasions, I have mentioned that we plan the lessons we are to learn on Earth, and therefore accidents are not really accidents because everything has a purpose and an end. So with this concept in mind, could we say that our interaction with a perpetrator is fortuitous? We cannot know for sure, but we can consider the following scenario: before reincarnating a spirit makes a contract with another spirit to play the role of the perpetrator in its reincarnation, in order to learn a lesson or experience an emotion. Would that be possible? Yes, I have seen it on several occasions during sessions with my clients.

Human beings are more susceptible and defenseless during childhood. That is why most of the problems, traumas, and symptoms that we experience in adulthood come from there, since not having the critical mind fully developed, everything we experience goes directly to our subconscious mind, creating an association that activates the symptom or behavior pattern to certain events that may resemble what we experienced in childhood. So, if we think about who influenced us the most during our childhood, it is easy to answer: our parents.

Through them, some of us have suffered abuse, rape, inappropriate touching, abandonment, denial, rejection, among other emotions—series of situations that simply turned us into their victims and consequently turned them into our perpetrators. So, going back to the concept that we plan our lessons and choose our birthplace and the type of body that will best lend itself to what we are to experience, remember that we also choose our parents and make a contract with them. Therefore, is the perpetrator a bad spirit or simply a spirit that will play that role in our lives to help us in our own spiritual evolution?

In conversations with spirits through their loved ones in hypnotic trance, we have been told that they passed away when they had to pass away, regardless of whether the death was from natural causes, a car accident, or murder. On the other hand, mediums I know who have received messages from spirits to be delivered to their still incarnated relatives expressed the same thing. I have never received a communication from a spirit condemning its perpetrator. What does this mean then?

Now, if we talk about karma, or the law of balance par excellence, which says that the person (spirit) that caused harm to another will have to experience the same thing that made them feel that way and with the same or greater intensity, we would have to pause to think how this spirit will be able to experience the same thing, how it will pay off that debt. Wouldn't it be through a perpetrator? And if this is so, wouldn't this be planned? Just remember the case of the woman I spoke about a few paragraphs ago, who in a past life was a soldier rapist and who in this life had to experience the same pain she had caused her victims, through different perpetrators at different times in her life.

Regardless of the motives that led a perpetrator to inflict pain on their victim, from the point of view of spirituality, both have and will have repercussions for this event. The offender may be affected in the future by the impact of the karma he himself generated, making him a victim, or at the end of his life when he realizes the pain he caused others. He may repent and feel that he does not deserve to be forgiven or to be happy in any other incarnation, becoming a victim who will play this role until he realizes the harm he is causing himself.

Every victim has been a perpetrator before. Therefore, when I come across a client seeking help and who is stuck in the victim role, it is only a matter of looking for the origin of when this victim was a perpetrator in order to help them end their pattern of self-sabotage.

The Observer

According to the definition that appears in dictionaries, the observer is one who watches or observes a thing or a person with great attention in order to acquire some information about their behavior or characteristics. From the therapeutic point of view, we refer to the observer as the person who witnesses an event before which they feel completely helpless, but who will be affected physically, mentally, or emotionally as a result of it.

A few lines above I referred to the childhood stage as the one in which we are most vulnerable to our environment, which is usually our family. For example, if an alcoholic father returns home drunk and unloads his anger and frustrations against his young children, they will be totally helpless and vulnerable in this situation and will feel like victims of their father. But what if we change the scenario such that when the father arrives home drunk, he takes out his anger and frustration on his wife while his children watch it all. This scenario turns those children into helpless observers, and they are and will be affected by what they are witnessing.

The role of observer is not only played by us in this life, but we have played it in other lives and may still be affected by it in the current life. An example might be that of a person who returns to a life in which he was a Nazi soldier who witnessed the mistreatment of the Jews and with which he disagreed, but about which he could do nothing because then it was his life that would be in danger. During that time he had no choice but to observe what seemed to him unjust and inhumane without being able to do or say anything about it. Although this soldier was not a victim of this mistreatment, by being its observer, he was being disturbed in an indirect way, becoming an indirect victim.

As Jose Luis Cabouli once explained to me, there is also the intelligent observer who knows that there is nothing he can do about what is happening because the perpetrator is at a less advanced level of evolution. No matter what I say or do to them, there will be no change. This intelligent observer then decides not to let what he is observing affect him.

There are very few occasions when these intelligent observers come to therapy as these events were usually not traumatic for their level of understanding and spiritual evolution. On the contrary, it is the powerless observer, the one who felt frustration or fear while witnessing the event, who ended up as affected as the victims themselves, but in an indirect way. The observer, like the victim, will experience the symptoms when they are triggered when confronted with a situation or emotion similar to the one that was stored in their subconscious mind, regardless of when it took place.

Many times, the observer will feel guilt, remorse, helplessness, and lack of self-confidence for no apparent reason in their current life. I still remember what was experienced by a young woman I met at a social event who was interested in understanding what hypnosis is. I asked her if she would be interested in doing a couple of exercises to determine how easy it was for her to go into trance, and she agreed.

The young woman went into a deep hypnotic trance very quickly, and at that point I began to take her back in time little by little to her childhood, even to the time when she was a baby. I continued to go back in time and from one moment to the next, she was in her mother's womb. As I began to ask her some questions, she began to scream uncontrollably, holding her hands to her ears, as if to avoid listening and saying, "Shut up! I can't take it anymore!" As I asked her what she was referring to, she told me that her grandmother was yelling at her mother and reproaching her for getting pregnant. What am I trying to express with this case? That we can also play the role of observer while in the womb, where everything we experience will affect us directly, even after we are born.

The Village Guard

To better capture how the roles of victim, perpetrator, and observer in a past life can affect us in the present, I will refer to Chris' session. He returned to my office to continue working on the symptoms he had.

Among the symptoms he brought to this second session were the insecurity and lack of self-confidence that had manifested itself throughout his life. This was accompanied by anxiety attacks and a tendency to avoid confrontation. He also told me that he was easily overwhelmed.

Antonio: What do you feel when you feel overwhelmed?

Chris: Pain.

A: And where do you feel that pain?

C: In my mind.

A: And what does that pain feel like that's going on in your mind?

C: Like I'm tired of it all.

A: Now I will count from three to one, and you will go to the moment when you are getting tired of it all. Three, two, one. You're already there. Where are you now? What's going on while you're getting tired of it all?

C: I see a lot of sand and it's very hot.

A: Look at your feet. What are you wearing?

C: Brown boots, like a farmer's boots.

A: Now touch your body. Is it a male or female?

C: Male.

A: Young or old?

C: Young.

A: What are you wearing?

C: A brown coat with a hood. I feel like I'm wearing something like a shield, like light armor.

A: Look around you. What place is that?

C: It's a village with wooden huts.

A: And if you knew, what are you doing there?

C: It's where I live, it's a small village. There are people walking through it. I'm guarding the area, making sure there are no intruders. I'm guarding the village.

A: Okay, go on a little bit more. What's happening now?

C: Someone comes to the entrance of the village, and I'm holding a spear. There are other guards with me. We are at the front of the village as this man approaches. We stop him and ask him what he is doing here. He says he is just passing through.

A: What's going on?

C: He is bringing food. He is a trader, and he brings them in his cart. He stops in the center of the village and people buy whatever he has from him.

A: That's right, go on some more.

C: Some are getting sick from the food. It's like a disease.

A: What kind of food is this?

C: It looks like pears. Some people are starting to die, and we thought they were poisoned.

A: Continue.

C: We can't find the man.

A: Continue.

C: We have found him behind a house. He has a long piece of wood and is being beaten by some people for some reason. I yell at him, telling him what is going on, and ask him why people are getting sick with the food. He says it is in revenge for what we did to his people.

A: And if you knew, what did you do to his people?

C: We were at war with his people.

A: What happens next?

C: I explode in anger and pierce his throat with the spear, killing him.

A: And what do you do next?

C: I feel that it's all my fault.

This would be the precise moment when Chris' spirit, incarnated in the body of the guard in that life, becomes a victim. He feels guilty for the death of his people because he was the guardian who was supposed to protect them.

C: Now I am taking his horse and going to his village, galloping for about 20 minutes. I am upset and sad because my people have died. I should have been the one to inspect the wagon to protect the villagers [again expressing his guilt].

A: So what happens now?

C: I am at the entrance of their village shouting. I drive my spear into the entrance of the village, declaring war on them.

A: So now they are at war again?

C: Yes, I'm going to make them pay. I am starting a fire in their village.

The entrance and the houses are starting to burn, and I see innocent people being hurt.

A: So what happens then?

C: It doesn't make me feel any better. I ride away, but I don't go back to my village. I'm leaving.

A: Why aren't you going back to your village?

C: Because I feel I have betrayed them, and now that I have burned a village to the ground and hurt innocent people for revenge, I feel I must never be seen again.

Chris had gone from being the victim of the one who poisoned the people in his village to being a victimizer when he not only killed that man in revenge, but burned his entire village. With the phrase "I think I must never be seen again," Chris returned once more to the role of victim, which would follow him into his present life generating the symptoms we already know.

A: So let's move to the last moment of that life.

C: I'm in the desert dying of dehydration. I can't go on.

A: Up to this point, what has been the most difficult moment in that life?

C: The betrayal of my humanity.

A: And when you are betraying your humanity, what are your physical reactions?

C: I feel abandoned and isolated.

A: And what are your physical reactions?

C: Not feeling anything.

A: And your mental reactions?

C: My life is torture.

A: Now I want you to see how all this is affecting your life as Chris. All this being abandoned and isolated, not feeling anything and feeling like your life is torture, what does that make you do in your life as Chris?

C: Avoiding everyone, not letting myself be seen.

A: What does this stop you from doing?

C: Continue with my life.

After the session, Chris was able to understand how all this that he thought and said in the guard's life was affecting him in his current life. With Chris' example we can clearly see how he went through the three roles and how they affected him in different ways.

First, he went through the role of observer as he watched the members of his village die without being able to do anything about it. Then, when he realized that the person he had let into the village had brought in poisoned food to take revenge, the guard changed from observer to feeling like a victim of the situation. Then, when he killed the man and went to seek revenge, burning the village in turn, he changed from victim to perpetrator. When the guard realized what he had done and the suffering he had caused to innocent people, he began to think of a series of commands that would bring his spirit back to the role of victim and then bring him back to Chris' life, feeling and behaving as he had pronounced in those commands.

The Woman Betrayed by the Council

Bernice scheduled a session to work on certain symptoms she had been experiencing: feeling like a victim, memory loss, and lack of joy in life. Her session began with a very mild trance, but gradually as she told me about her sad memories, Bernice became more connected, allowing her to experience everything more deeply.

Initially she visited a memory in which, due to a family event, she had felt betrayed. So I decided to explore this emotion further, as I perceived that it was related to the symptoms she had brought to the session.

Antonio: Bernice, I want you to go to the first moment when you felt betrayed. Allow your body and soul to feel whatever they need to feel. Five, four, three, two, one. You are already there. Tell me whatever comes to your mind, even if you think you are imagining it. Look at your feet. What are you wearing?

Bernice: I don't know if I'm barefoot or if I'm wearing some kind of flat sandals.

A: Does the body feel male or female?

B: I'm a woman. I'm climbing the stairs outside something that looks like a pyramid. I have been called to a council.

A: So you are climbing the stairs?

B: Yes, I am climbing the stairs.

A: And how do you feel as you go up?

B: I feel confident, but a little nervous.

A: And while you're with that council, what's going on?

B: They are asking me questions. I think they have betrayed me.

A: Why have they betrayed you? Why do you think they are doing it?

B: Because they have something to gain from it.

A: Let your body feel betrayed. What are they saying?

B: They are accusing me of having done something, but it is not true.

A: How does it make you feel?

B: Sad, I feel something in my stomach again. I think it's making me nauseous [showing discomfort on her face]. It's making it hard to breathe.

A: Feel that some more. Why do you think it's hard to breathe?

B: I have pressure in my lungs [starting to breathe more deeply].

A: What else is going on? Come forward a little more.

B: I think they want to kill me.

A: And why are you having trouble breathing? Let your body feel everything.

B: I think they gave me something to drink. I feel my stomach tense. I trusted them, I really trusted them. I wanted something very much.

A: So far, what has been the most difficult moment of this experience?

B: Feeling betrayed. I trusted them so much... I trusted them so much.

A: I'm going to count from three to one, and you'll go to the moment when you're taking that thing they gave you, the moment when you've been betrayed. Three, two, one. You are already there. Let your body feel everything. What is happening now?

B: They have given me something to drink. I've been told that if I take this, something is going to happen, that I'm going to have powers or something.

A: And while you are drinking that, what are your physical reactions?

B: My abdomen, my stomach, my intestines—everything is burning. I'm very nauseous and I can't breathe properly. What have they given me? [stretching her neck, showing that she couldn't get enough air].

A: That's it, feel that even more.

I hadn't finished telling her that when suddenly her body arched up on the bed, bringing her hand to her chest and neck as she opened her mouth to breathe. Bernice had returned to the moment when she had been poisoned, and her body was experiencing it again. She could see how, from one moment to the next, she no longer had control over the experience and her body was reacting on its own.

B: Oh, God!" [with a pained and frightened expression].

A: That's right, what are your emotional reactions?

B: Why did you do this to me? [after a few seconds of silence, while still trying to breathe].

A: And what are your mental reactions?

B: Why am I being killed? It's so sad. My head hurts.

A: And while that body is dying, what is the last thought you manage to think in that brain?

B: What did I do wrong? What have I done to deserve this?

A: Alright, now I'm going to count from five to one, and I want you to go back to the moment when you're taking that. Allow your body to feel everything again. Five, four, three, two, one. You're already there. [I instructed, when suddenly Bernice began to writhe in pain again.]

A: While you're taking that, what is your stomach feeling?

B: It hurts.

A: And what's your throat feeling?

B: It's closed. I can't breathe. I can't talk either [she answered tearfully].

A: How do your lungs feel?

B: I can't get any air.

A: What does the heart feel?

B: It is red and very big.

A: What does the brain feel?

B: My brain hurts so much.

A: And how is all of this affecting you in your life as Bernice?

B: I can't express myself; I can't digest food.

A: And when you can't express yourself or digest food, what does that make you do?

B: I don't express whether something is right or wrong. I don't express my feelings. I have a lot of difficulty remembering events. My brain is blocking a lot of memories and feelings. If I don't have memories and feelings, I can't express myself. The poison has damaged my nervous system.

A: When you are ready, get out of that body understanding that with the death of that body that experience is over forever, and it is not going to affect you anymore. That's it, very good. Now I want you to talk to those who killed you. What do you want to tell them?

When I said this, Bernice started coughing, clearly showing that she was still being affected by the poison.

A: I want you to turn on your side and vomit up the poison they gave you. It's going to be an energetic vomit. [I told her this so she could vomit out the energetic charge that poison left in her soul.]

Bernice began to cough more deeply, making sounds as if she was actually vomiting the poison.

A: Get that poison out of your system. That's it!

B: My throat is clear [she said with great relief].

A: Now that you are out of the body, talk to these people and tell them everything you have wanted to tell them all this time.

B: Why did you betray me, what did I do wrong?

A: Ask them to give you back your energy, the one they took from you when they killed you.

B: Give me back my energy! I want it now. It is mine. You had no right to kill me. I want all my power back.

A: When you are ready, stretch out your arms and bring all your energy back.

The navigation through that life ended after the evaluation of the lessons to be learned. Bernice had found the experience that had caused her to feel like a victim and to feel betrayed. We had also found the root of her digestive problems, which had been generated by ingesting the poison.

Other consequences of the poisoning were the problems she had with memory loss and not being able to express herself. The poison was still negatively influencing her soul on an energetic level. By reliving the death of that body, she was able to become aware of everything that happened at that time on a physical, emotional, and mental level, ending with the entrapment of her soul.

CONCLUSION

Human beings are marvelous and complex beings. Each one of us is like a universe that lives within another universe, which in turn is part of other universes. If we only focus our attention on the human body, we will face what the spiritualist André Luiz described as 'the divine machine,' which consists of organs as varied and extraordinary as the microscopic elements that live inside us—in short, a whole universe within a body created to perfection.

If we focus on the soul, or the incarnated spirit, we will realize that it is energy with consciousness that is integrated into the physical body, to that universe contained within itself, to experience and evolve on this planet. The soul is a multidimensional being, that is it can exist not only inside the body but also outside of it in other higher dimensions to which it gets as it learns. Moreover, the incarnated soul does not remain inside the body all the time. For example, when the body sleeps, it visits other dimensions to continue interacting and experiencing with other souls. Some people do this without being conscious, but others do it at will, in what is known as astral projection.

Both the human body and the soul have their own history. We can find that of the physical body through the genes that are passed down from generation to generation. These are what will give the body unique characteristics that will work both for and against the spirit that inhabits it when it is created. The history of the soul can be found in its reincarnations, in the experiences accumulated in other bodies it occupied in past lives.

Then the union of body and soul at the moment of reincarnation will conceive a unique and perfect being for learning. That spirit that carefully chose its body before reincarnating made sure to create an environment favorable to experience, interact, and learn what it planned in the spirit world. But where does the challenge lie then? The soul, trapped in those traumatic events that it could not fully process on a physical, emotional, and mental level—that is, where it could not do all that was to be done before the death of the body—will cause these unfinished events to manifest in the new body in the form of physical, emotional, and mental symptoms.

Based on this idea, should symptoms be treated by focusing only on the physical body? Or similarly, should mental disorders be treated solely from the point of view of the mind? I think not, for to help a person who is experiencing unexplained discomfort, whether physical, emotional, or mental, we must look at the human being and the spirit as a whole, unraveling the history of both as a whole.

The soul holds all the information we need. That is why the hypnosis techniques I use are oriented to the soul, since I find in it a great repository of experiences in different bodies. Then, once we understand what the soul experienced, either in a previous body or at the moment of detachment from it, during its passage through the mother's womb, birth, early childhood, or even later in life, we can decipher the origin and explanation of the symptom in order to help the individual in the best possible way. Thus, they will be able to continue with their spiritual evolution.

The symptom is only the tip of the iceberg, the only conscious thing for the human being, but it is associated with an experience excluded from the conscious mind. We could say that if the symptoms are icebergs, the events that trigger them are at the bottom of the sea. It is on them that we must turn our attention to help the soul to heal.

As the soul walks the path to its evolution, it reincarnates again and again without ceasing to learn lessons and experience all kinds of events that will direct it to its evolutionary goal. It is in this constant return to

Earth that, by not processing these events and lessons fully, part of our soul and energy becomes trapped, causing each future body we occupy to suffer the symptoms caused by this entrapment.

That is why I consider it vital that every therapist bases their techniques and sessions on spirituality, helping these incarnated souls to end their entrapment and do everything they were unable to do in order to free them of all burden. I also believe that every therapist who wishes to embark on this mission of helping others must develop qualities such as patience, compassion, love for others and non-judgment. The path ahead of them will be winding and full of challenges, for they themselves, in guiding their own clients, will have to heal their own wounds, their own symptoms.

Never pity or feel sorry for the patient who comes to our doors. Never focus on the physical body in front of us, but on the soul that inhabits it and that came to us seeking healing and guidance. Love and compassion will always be the best tools we can use.

THE SYMPTOMS OF
THE SOUL

THE PATH TO THE ORIGIN OF OUR SYMPTOMS
THROUGH REGRESSIVE HYPNOSIS

www.ingramcontent.com/pod-product-compliance
Lightning Source LLC
Chambersburg PA
CBHW071739150426
43191CB00010B/1629